72 Questions (and Answers) About Life and Becoming the Man God Designed You to Be

Tim Shoemaker and Mark Shoemaker

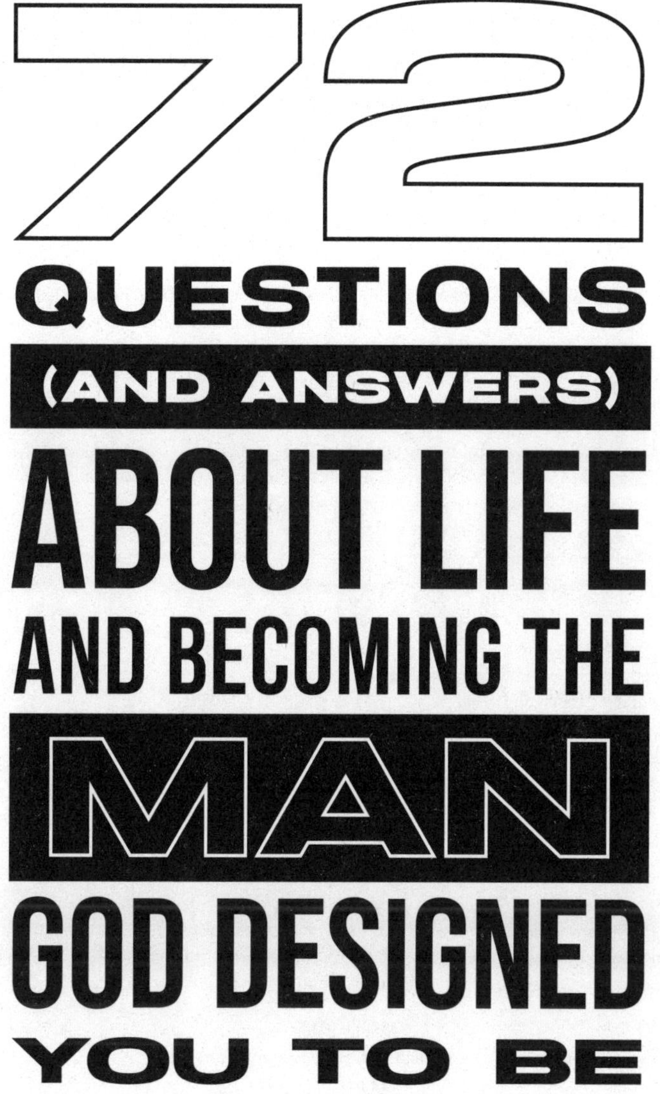

72 QUESTIONS (AND ANSWERS) ABOUT LIFE AND BECOMING THE MAN GOD DESIGNED YOU TO BE

TIM SHOEMAKER AND MARK SHOEMAKER

MOODY PUBLISHERS
CHICAGO

Emphasis to Scripture has been added.

Cyle Young Literary Elite, LLC

Edited by Pamela Joy Pugh
Interior design: Faceout Studio, Paul Nielson
Cover design: Thinkpen Design
Cover graphic of arrow copyright © 2025 by N.Petrosyan/Shutterstock (2490794477).
All rights reserved.
Author photos: Emma Kuntz (emmafinlayson.com)

ISBN: 978-0-8024-3623-8

Originally delivered by fleets of horse-drawn wagons, the affordable paperbacks from D. L. Moody's publishing house resourced the church and served everyday people. Now, after more than 125 years of publishing and ministry, Moody Publishers' mission remains the same—even if our delivery systems have changed a bit. For more information on other books (and resources) created from a biblical perspective, go to www.moodypublishers.com or write to:

Moody Publishers
820 N. LaSalle Boulevard
Chicago, IL 60610

1 3 5 7 9 10 8 6 4 2

Printed in the United States of America

To Caleb, James, Miles, Daniel, Ethan, and Gabe. Some of the most important things I want to convey to you about manhood are written in this book.

And to my readers . . . boys who have grown up loving the Code of Silence and High Water series. I've loved being part of your life . . . and the journey isn't over. This book is a next step.

—Tim

To all those I've sat in conversation with across a table or a firepit about the types of things we cover in this book. Some of these topics here were born out of our talks together. As I wrote, I pictured you . . . especially my big three . . . and you know who you are.

If even one part makes a difference in your life, it will be worth every effort writing it.

—Mark

"Hear, my son, and accept my words,
that the years of your life may be many.
I have taught you the way of wisdom;
I have led you in the paths of uprightness.
When you walk, your step will not be hampered,
and if you run, you will not stumble.
Keep hold of instruction; do not let go;
guard her, for she is your life." Proverbs 4:10–13

CONTENTS

Out of the Ditch

I (Tim) spotted the pickup and instantly knew the driver was in deep weeds. Somehow, he'd lost control and slid off the exit ramp going from westbound I-90 to northbound Route 53. Unintentional off-roading. Now the F-150 was a good 120 feet down a steep embankment—and dangerously close to a nasty-looking ditch at the bottom. I pulled over and hustled toward his truck.

The ground was hash-marked with tire ruts that he'd created while trying to get back up to the ramp. Some of the furrows were deep enough to plant corn. He gunned the gas and tried climbing again. Dirt and sod clumps went flying. He fishtailed—but wasn't getting traction. The F-150 slid backward—and he stood on the brake. By the time the truck stopped, he was even closer to the ditch than before.

Dread. Fear. Panic. I'm pretty sure I saw all these in his eyes as I approached the driver's door. He was young. Eighteen maybe?

He rolled down his window. He explained that he'd taken a friend and his family to Chicago's O'Hare Airport, and they'd insisted he drive their truck. All he had to do was park it in their garage afterward—which wasn't going to happen now. "I called a tow truck, but they said it could be an hour."

The wrecker would need at least fifty yards of steel cable and a powerful winch if it was going to pull him out. I eyed the pickup, and the steep grade it needed to climb. Hey, it was an F-150, right? I was sure it could make the ascent—if it was done just right. I was pretty sure I could talk him into letting me drive the truck. He looked plenty desperate. But what he really needed was to drive that thing himself, with a little help.

"Okay, I think you can do this without a tow truck. How about I walk alongside you and give you some advice along the way. You up for that?"

He nodded. Like I said, he looked desperate.

"We're going up at too steep of an angle to climb this." I placed my hand on the driver's door, right where I'd rest my elbow if I were driving a sweet truck like this down the highway. "So, we need to drop it in neutral, ease off the brake, and cut the wheel my way. We're going to have to let the truck roll backward to get into a better position."

Doubt was all over his face at the idea of letting the truck roll even farther from the ramp. To his credit, he gave me a nod and a look that said *I'm trusting you . . . please don't let me down.*

"Nice and easy now. Keep your foot on the brake, but we're going to feather it a little."

He executed it nicely but kept his eyes on me instead of the rearview mirror. We rolled a whole lot closer to the ditch before the truck was angled the way it needed to be.

"Brakes."

He didn't say a word. Only after he'd stopped did he check his rearview.

"You're doing good. Turn your wheels the other way." I did a clockwise circle with my hand, stopping him when the angle looked right.

His eyes were locked on me again.

"Okay . . . now we'll do this together. You're going to give it a little gas." I pointed up the embankment at a long angle. "And head for that mile marker on the shoulder—way over there."

He licked dry lips. Nodded. Took a deep breath. Tightened his death-grip on the wheel.

"Here we go."

The tires spun, then got their traction, and the truck eased forward.

"A little more gas."

He hunkered over the wheel. The F-150 picked up speed.

"Good. You're doing it. Keep the wheel right there." I trotted alongside the truck now, my hand still on the door. The incline was getting steeper. "Don't slow up. Give it just a bit more gas. Keep your eye on that mile marker."

He followed through perfectly.

"Keep going . . . you've got this. Right up to the top." He was moving faster than I was now. I dropped off and watched the F-150 claw its way to the shoulder and park on level ground.

He swung out of the cab and ran back to meet me, his face bright with relief—and pride. "We did it! How'd you know how to do that? Thanks, man!"

It was a great moment—for him and for me. When I'd first approached him, I'm sure he wondered if I'd be able to help. But he trusted I knew what I was doing, or he was desperate enough to take the chance that I'd actually be able to help. Now he'd park that truck in his friend's garage without a scratch on it. He'd just dodged a towing bill and didn't have the embarrassment of an apologetic call to his friend's dad. Better still was the elation on his face. With a little coaching, he'd just accomplished something that might have worked for a "built Ford tough" commercial.

There are plenty of very good books available that talk about God's design for manhood. What a man is—or isn't. Books that do a terrific job of clearing up some of the gender confusion in today's world. Books that clarify a man's roles. Read them, for sure. Sometimes great books about manhood give you something to celebrate, but after finishing that read, you still feel a bit like you're in a ditch—and you're not sure how to get out.

This book is more about what to do *next*. How does this manhood thing work? What are some very real steps I can take toward the tough job of becoming the man God designed me to be? Manhood can be a rugged, uphill climb. Lots of guys lose traction, flip over, or end up in a ditch. That doesn't have to happen to you. We want to help.

We're a father (Tim) and son (Mark) team here. Collectively, we've put a bunch of miles on the odometer of life. We've experienced—seen—so much of what it takes to be a man. And we want to share this with you.

We're not asking you to move over and give us the wheel. Just let us run alongside you for a bit and offer some suggestions.

I'm asking you to trust us a little—and the truth of God's Word a whole lot. Take these things we'll be sharing with you for a little test drive. See if you don't find yourself getting traction like you never did before. Do that, and by the time you finish this book, I think you'll find yourself on much more level ground—and maybe even up to highway speeds!

Roll down your window, my friend, and let's get started.

—Tim and Mark

SECTION
ONE

THE FOUNDATIONAL FIVE

I (Tim) took an advanced scuba class recently, which included deep water diving and underwater navigation. The in-water testing portion was down in the Florida Keys. Just before the deep-water test, I sat in the dive boat with my mind looping through everything I needed to remember. The test meant descending to a Navy ship sitting on the bottom over a hundred feet below me. At that depth, there isn't much margin for error. A mistake can be seriously costly.

And there would be distractions. The wreck itself would be fascinating. And the area was also known to have strong currents—and sharks. How would I take in the sights, keep an eye out for the dangers, and remember all the other things I'd learned in class? It was way too much. And once I started my descent to the ocean floor, it would be too late to ask questions.

The thing I realized? There were only a handful of things I absolutely *had* to stay focused on for this dive. My depth. The amount of air in my tank. My no-decompression stop time. Staying with my dive buddy. Keeping my eye on the instructor. Five things. I could do that. And as long as I did, everything else would fall in line.

When we think of manhood, we could talk about tons of things. *So* many, that you might be feeling the same thing I did on that dive boat. *How can I remember it all?* The truth is only a handful of things are essential for this dive into manhood—but you'll need every one of them, as together, they form a foundation. Everything else in the book builds on one or more of these five. Everything you need for becoming the man God designed you to be hinges on your understanding and mastery of these five things:

- ✓ Living out God's purpose
- ✓ Self-control
- ✓ Holy Spirit–control
- ✓ Abiding in Christ
- ✓ Putting God's Word into practice

Let's take a brief look at each one.

FOUNDATIONAL FIVE
#1: Living Out God's Purpose

This phase of life in as a young man in is critical . . . where you'll make some of the most important and best decisions of your life—or some major mistakes. These next few years are when tons of guys mess up their life, and some never recover. Some guys develop dangerous habits and form incorrect views, ignoring the principles, commands, and wisdom in God's Word. They do things they'd be ashamed to tell their parents or grandparents about—all in a futile pursuit of making themselves happy.

If life is so important and such a gift—and it is—there must be more to it than the shallow goal of making ourselves happy. The truth is that were created by God. We're *His* project. And that means that decisions about our future aren't ours alone to make. We are not the captain of our own ship.

But actually, many guys go through life thinking they *are* the captain of their own ship. Doing things our way was how we originally got into trouble. Anytime we do something apart from God's way, it's called sin—and our sin has consequences.

Sin separates us from having a relationship with God, both on earth and for eternity. There's nothing we can do on our own to change our standing with God; our life purpose can't ever reach beyond the destruction of our sin.

But God offers us a way out: a new life where we get to live for His purpose instead of chasing our own. When Jesus died on the cross, He paid the price of our sin by taking on the punishment we deserved for doing things our way. If we put our faith in Jesus, we receive God's gift of forgiveness. He saves us from our sin and gives us a new life spiritually. We are no longer living under the control of sin and chasing our own personal happiness and ambitions. We now live totally for God . . . and His purposes in our life.

And we find life is much better that way.

It all starts there. In fact, everything in this book is built on our having that relationship with God through Jesus. Those who reject Jesus end up on the rocks. They'll captain their ship all right—all the way to hell.

That's not what we want for you.

"For we are his workmanship, created in Christ Jesus for good works, which God prepared beforehand, that we should walk in them" (Ephesians 2:10).

You were created, by God, for His purposes. There are things that He designed you to do. A destiny He has uniquely gifted you for. It may not be the life you expected or dreamed of or even imagined, but it's a life that will resonate deep in your soul. A life that will cause you to say over and over and over—*I was made for this.*

So, this is the first to remember: God created you for a purpose. He wants you to have right standing with Him through His Son, Jesus, and live a life pleasing to Him.

Make this decision. Talk to God about it. Tell Him you want to be the man He designed you to be and do the things He's made you to do. Realize that sometimes God needs to change things about you so you can become the man God designed you to be. That's okay, because there's nothing more fulfilling and exciting!

FOUNDATIONAL FIVE
#2: Self-Control Is Possible

If you're a follower of Christ, the enemy wants to take you out.

So many young men leave high school like one of those moving ducks in a county fair shooting gallery. With no cover, no protection, they're easy targets. As men, we need walls of protection from our enemy. And the best walls aren't made with stone or concrete; they're built through self-control.

Self-control is about consistently doing the right, best thing even when we don't feel like it. Even when nobody is watching. Even when we *really* want to do something else. It's choosing to live out the wisdom God gives us in His Word—even when we have the opportunity to do or say something we might find *way* more gratifying at the moment. Self-control isn't limited to the things we do, but also the things we say. The places we let our minds wander.

"A man without self-control is like a city broken into and left without walls" (Proverbs 25:28).

Think about a city without walls in Bible times. An enemy army could march right in with nothing to stop them. A man who lived in a city without walls couldn't protect himself. And get this . . . he couldn't protect the ones he loved. Nobody in a city without walls is safe.

This verse in Proverbs gives us an important secret to manhood. A man must have walls of self-control in place if he is to be safe—and if he wants to keep others safe. Without walls of self-control, we're vulnerable. If we don't learn to consistently say no to things we know are wrong, we're making our enemy's job easy.

Why do young men struggle with this? Why is self-control so difficult—and so underdeveloped in men?

Self-control requires self-denial, something we don't have to do very often in our lives. The convenience of our society means we rarely have to say no to ourselves. That weakens our development of self-control.

Click a button and receive your purchase on your doorstep the next day.

Open that app and have endless streaming entertainment.

We have a buffet of options that allow us to regularly say yes to our desires. This produces habits that are bent toward ease, comfort, instant gratification, and convenience. None of those words would be used to describe someone with strong walls of self-control.

What helps you develop these strong walls?

- Create boundaries, lines you won't cross. Then, when you're faced with temptation or the need to make a quick decision, you'll already know what to do.
- Tell friends, parents, your girlfriend (or wife), other trustworthy men the walls you want to put up and why.
- Most important, tell God about the walls you want to build. Ask Him to help you build them—and to stay within them.

Self-control is about building habits so that when you're in a situation of high temptation, danger, or requiring a quick decision, you'll automatically do the right thing.

Walls of self-control don't hold you back from fun. They keep you alive so you can have fun for years to come—and most importantly—so you can live out God's good plans for your life.

FOUNDATIONAL FIVE
#3: Holy Spirit–Control

Be all you can be.

We've often heard these words, haven't we? The idea is that we shouldn't settle for being less of a man than we could be with some dedicated effort. The slogan encourages us to dig deeper, try harder, and bring out the best in ourselves. Sure, with some effort we can kick bad habits, be kinder, more considerate—and generally become a more decent man.

But the idea of reaching within ourselves to become a better person is deeply flawed. There isn't a better version of us deep inside. Honestly? We have a bent to live selfishly and love wrong things.

The good man that we want to become isn't found within ourselves but comes after true surrender to the Holy Spirit. Take a look at what God wants to grow in us through the Holy Spirit: "Love, joy, peace, patience, kindness, goodness, faithfulness, gentleness, self-control" (Galatians 5:22–23). Can you imagine the man you'd be if these attributes were a growing part of your life?

It's easy to compare ourselves with people around us and think we're okay—good enough. We can become satisfied with our progress and call that the finish line. But unless we already look like Jesus—in every way—the Spirit still has work to do within us.

The more He changes us, the more rewarding it is for us and everyone around us. We should look different this year than we did last year. Those changes should be obvious to us, and to those around us as well.

So, how do we allow the Holy Spirit to have more control in our life?

- It starts in our heart. We need to *want* to be controlled by the Holy Spirit.
- Next, surrender. We ask the Holy Spirit to change us. To rework our desires. To show us where we need to change—and help us do that.

This isn't a one-and-done kind of thing. Count on this being a daily prayer.

Say you're frustrated about something or with someone. Likely the thoughts and emotions and maybe even the words or actions coming out of you don't fit that love, joy, peace, patience, kindness, goodness, faithfulness, gentleness, and self-control that typifies the work of the Holy Spirit.

To be the kind of man God has designed us to be, we're going to need some supernatural assistance. Try a simple prayer like this one: "Lord, I'm feeling frustrated/angry/wronged (fill in the emotion) right now. A big part of me feels I'm right, that I'm justified for feeling that way. But I know if I keep going the way I'm headed, I'm going to make a mess. I'll do or say something that would be wrong. So, I'm asking You to help me. I'm submitting to You, asking You to change my mind and heart like only You can."

We might not receive an instant and complete change of heart. More likely we'll get a tiny change of perspective. Like a door has cracked open just a bit. We gain a slightly different view of the situation—or of the person. And that's enough. Because at that moment, our job is to push through that opening.

These things we struggle with likely have to do with our past, our habits or our old nature. Having a hard time loving or forgiving someone else. Anger. Frustration. Lust. Pride. Selfishness. Jealousy.

But over time, as we continue to ask the Holy Spirit for help, the old nature has less of a hold on our life. The Holy Spirit is creating heart change in us. Things that once seemed hard or impossible—like forgiving others—become incredibly easier and entirely doable, because you've invited God to change your heart and you acted on what you were to do.

As a result of this heart change, our life becomes filled with more and more of the good things that the Spirit produces in those surrendered to Him. Love. Joy. Peace. Kindness. Self-control. These are amazingly good things that we want in our life as men, so let's pursue this Holy Spirit–control thing with everything in us.

You'll find that this absolutely works. Without this, you'll find the Christian life—and becoming the man God designed you to be—impossible.

Sometimes people chalk up their anger, attitude, selfishness as "just who I am." As followers of Jesus, we're given the Holy Spirit to impact and change *all* of who we are. Our existing character or personality is just God's starting point.

FOUNDATIONAL FIVE
#4: Abiding in Christ

We don't use the word "abiding" very often. It simply means *remaining*. Jesus wants us to remain attached and receive from Him. But how do we do that—and what does that even look like? The best way to abide is by deciding to spend time with God each day. When we spend time in His Word or pray, we receive nutrients that help us grow spiritual fruit, just like the vine and branches.

How can we possibly be abiding in Jesus if we're not spending intentional time with Him that includes Bible reading and prayer?

Have you thought this? "I don't have time to read my Bible or sit and pray." The real reason we don't spend time with God isn't because we're too busy. It's because we don't know how important it is. Or, we think we're doing okay because we go to church—or we're serving there, or we don't do the "big" sins that others do. We conclude that we're doing all right, we don't *need* more.

Or we think of time with God as something we'll get to later . . . as if we'll wake up one day and suddenly have more time to give to God. I'll break it to you now; life doesn't slow down. You won't have a better opportunity in your life to build the habit of spending time with God than you have right now.

So how do we do this abiding? For all of us our time with God could sometimes be described as confusing and distracted. Afterward, we honestly wonder . . . did that do anything? We don't see our own time with God as being fruitful or beneficial, so we resign ourselves to just being fed on the weekend at church.

I'm convinced, if we knew what God produces in us through our intentional time with Him, we would never miss it.

Check out what Jesus says about our need for Him: "Abide in me, and I in you. As the branch cannot bear fruit by itself, unless it abides in the vine, neither can you, unless you abide in me. I am the vine; you are the branches. Whoever abides in me and I in him, he it is that bears much fruit, for apart from me you can do nothing" (John 15:4–5).

Jesus explains that spiritual life blooms only through a relationship with Him. This begins the moment we are saved, but it doesn't stop there. It's also true of every moment of our life afterward. If we are going to grow and become more like Jesus, it requires a lifetime of abiding in Him, day by day. Every single good action/thought/motive is a result of what God is giving us and growing in us through the time we spend with Him.

Apart from Jesus, we will not grow, we will not overcome temptation, we will not know God deeper, we will lack hope when we're going through trials and suffering. There won't be good fruit on our branches. We need Him, desperately. Every day . . . all day.

If we detach and go at our day alone, the result isn't a mystery. A branch that is no longer connected to the vine won't produce fruit. And in time, the branch will lose all strength and rot away.

So will we. Just being in church—or around other Christians—isn't enough for us to grow.

So, what does a life of abiding look like?

Here are three things to help you abide today.

Make it enjoyable: Why do we often associate our time with God as a stuffy, formal event? Instead, let's go and make that time with God enjoyable, just like you'd do with a good friend. You like hiking? How can you build time in God's Word around that? You like coffee? Why not enjoy a cup while you hang out with God in the morning? Go read your Bible in your favorite spot. Have your prayer time while you (insert a hobby here). Our time with God is a relationship we are building, that should be an enjoyable experience!

Make it more than a time slot: How often do we see our time with God as a checklist? "I read that chapter in the Bible . . . my time with God is DONE!" The problem with that is that's not how abiding works. The vine remains all day and all night. Let's shift from seeing God as *part* of our day to viewing Him as with us *all day long*. To abide in the Vine, we need to connect all parts of our day to Him.

That car ride is an opportunity to be with God. So is that workout, or shower, or next load of laundry. Make a playlist with some of your favorite worship songs and find random times of your day to use them in worship (while you're getting ready in the morning, while you're driving, during passing periods, while you do homework). Listen to sermons during your week; there are many solid preachers and amazing podcasts. You might be surprised how a sermon keeps your conversation with God going.

Make it fresh: It's so easy to get into a rut of doing the same thing with God every day. But which relationship in your life do you ever hang out in the same way every single day? Think of some new ways to hang out with God—then try them!

Maybe something new for you would be a prayer journal. Or you could take walks and listen to the Bible on audio. Try something more intense, like fasting. Memorize Scripture. There are all sorts of ways to connect with God; which ones have you been missing out on?

John 15:11 is a mind-blowing verse. Right after talking about abiding, Jesus says, "These things I have spoken to you, that my joy may be in you, and that your joy may be full."

When I (Mark) lack joy, or feel far from God, or am struggling more with temptation, I check my abiding time. This is always my starting point. If that's off, likely everything else will be too.

The foundation of abiding leads to our next point, putting it all into practice. And that is where the fullness of joy Christ gives happens.

FOUNDATIONAL FIVE
#5: Putting God's Word into Practice

The Bible only records one of Jesus' sermons. And at the very end, I (Tim) believe Jesus reveals one of the greatest secrets to living a Christian life that is wise and actually works.

"Everyone then who hears these words of mine and does them will be like a wise man who built his house on the rock. And the rain fell, and the floods came, and the winds blew and beat on that house, but it did not fall, because it had been founded on the rock. And everyone who hears these words of mine and does not do them will be like a foolish man who built his house on the sand. And the rain fell, and the floods came, and the winds blew and beat against that house, and it fell, and great was the fall of it" (Matthew 7:24–27).

When we read these verses, we often focus on the two houses: the one on the rock and the one on the sand. But tucked in here is the important part: "Everyone who hears these words of mine *and does* them . . ." or "*does not do* them." Jesus pointed out that all the people who hear what He says can be broken down into just two groups: those who put His teaching into practice and those who don't.

We may have grown up in the church, attend every week, and know tons about the Bible. But that isn't enough to help us survive the storms of life. Knowing what the Bible says doesn't even mean that we're wise. To be considered wise, by Jesus' standards, is to put the Word into practice. To consistently do what it says. To make a habit of obeying the Word. As we read something in the Bible that we're to do—or to avoid—we take that to heart. We work at it. The Bible is our guide, yes . . . but that's only effective when we put it into practice.

When we put something into practice, it's about working on that. It's about getting better in that area. Keeping our focus on that. Sometimes it takes time to build new habits and break old ones. *We* work on it (self-control) and we ask *God* to help us (Holy Spirit–control).

Putting what He says into practice can mean many things. Here are a few:

Guarding our language; forgiving; praying for those who have hurt us; praying for direction; being an example to others; not arguing or complaining. You can fill in many more.

Putting the Word into practice is about taking deliberate action. If I read a passage on loving others, and walk away saying, "Okay, I need to love people better," I haven't taken any action—and I haven't been specific enough. I haven't established a way to measure whether I actually love people better. It would be wiser to clarify what it looks like to love others better. *Who* do I need to love better? *When* do I struggle to love others? *What* can I do this week to show love for ______________? Notice how all these questions direct me to very specific ways to apply the text. And if we don't apply those specific things, we'll know it right away. We'll easily identify where we missed the mark—and be able to make corrections.

Building a house on the sand—without a foundation—sounds like a pretty foolish and shortsighted thing to do . . . especially if hurricanes tend to sweep through the area. But there's something that would be even more devastating personally to us than that. Failing to put into practice what we read in the Bible. Let's not let that happen to us.

Now let's get started on some of the questions we face as men and how to become the man God created each of us to be.

SECTION
TWO

DATING

One thing I've (Mark) found that tends to sidetrack/derail/discourage/confuse young men in their walk with God more than anything else is dating. It's where so many guys face their strongest temptations—and end up compromising most. It's the most desired experience of young men, while simultaneously holding the deepest hurts and regrets. Guys seem to either be running toward dating or limping away from it.

Most of you, at some point these next years, will either pursue a dating relationship or find yourself in one. Let's talk about what it looks like to date well based on what the Bible teaches. Which is honestly a little tricky to do, because there isn't a verse on dating. In Bible times, their culture was actually less into dating and more into arranged marriages. Don't worry, that isn't going to be our official stance on dating here. Man, that would be a short chapter!

It's still possible to build a biblical framework for how we should date, which will guide us toward a dating experience that pleases God—and actually brings us closer to Him.

1
If There's One Thing I Really Need to Know About Dating, What Is It?

There are a lot of reasons guys ask a girl on a date. Fun. Experience. Status. Curiosity. She's attractive and you're enamored. Some of these things are part of why we date. It's totally understandable. But it becomes a problem when these things are *the reason* you're dating. Nothing on that list (and honestly that list could be so much longer) should be motivating us to get into a relationship. The real reason is simple but also intimidating. The purpose for dating is all about finding the right girl . . . the one you will marry.

We see this in the garden of Eden. No, Adam didn't date Eve. But their relationship is going to give us insight into how we should approach dating—and a relationship with a girl. You can read about it in Genesis 2:18–25 but allow me (Mark) to paraphrase. God had created Adam but made it clear that it wasn't good for Adam to be alone. It's not that God's creation was bad, just that He wasn't done yet. So, God announced that He was going to make a "helper fit for him."

Cue the controversy. Helper?! Doesn't that sound a bit demeaning? Well, *no*. The word *helper* is most commonly used in the Old Testament to refer to God Himself as the Helper to Israel. Eve isn't a helper like my toddler is my helper as I mow the lawn. Eve, as helper, is a necessity and benefit for Adam. Israel doesn't go into battle without their Helper, God of creation. Adam is best not to do life without his helper, Eve of Eden.

▪ ▪ ▪

Tim: The Bible also refers to the Holy Spirit as our "helper." A woman who has a heart for God is designed to be *that* kind of helper in many ways. My wife influences me to be more loving, kinder, and less selfish. She gives me insights on things and people so that I can make better decisions. She encourages me to be the man God designed me to be. Did you notice how her role is so integral, so valuable . . . and so similar to the Holy Spirit in my life? A guy who thinks a woman is to be his servant is missing so much that his wife *could* be—and what he'd be as a result.

▪ ▪ ▪

Adam sees Eve and is blown away. He's been naming animals and has seen beautiful creations, but none of it compares to what his eyes see now. "Bone of my bones and flesh of my flesh!" Adam is drawn to her. They experience intimacy and are pronounced "one flesh."

This is great (and likely familiar); but what does it have to do with dating? Well, a lot actually. It builds a foundation for how we think about relationships. God has created us as His image bearers, with the ability for oneness and intimacy with the opposite sex. It explains why we have such a deep longing for it! While there are many reasons people start to date, Genesis gives us the picture of what we were created to experience. It's the desire deep in our hearts we are actually searching for in relationships with a woman . . . *oneness.*

God's gift to Adam that day gives us our purpose in dating today. It's to find someone we can experience the love and bond God gave uniquely to us to enjoy within marriage. Our goal for dating should align with God's vision for male and female relationships in the garden.

So, it makes sense that we should only date women who we believe have the possibility of becoming our Eve/helper/wife. That's not to say that every dating relationship will end with marriage. Of course not. But every dating relationship sets finding the one to marry as the destination. If we start dating for any other reason, it will always lead us down a path the relationship wasn't meant to go.

Many women in our life will be great friends/teammates/sisters in Christ, and that's good and should be enjoyed. But only one becomes what God gave to Adam. If we keep that thought at the forefront of our relationships with women, it gives a good foundation for how we go about dating.

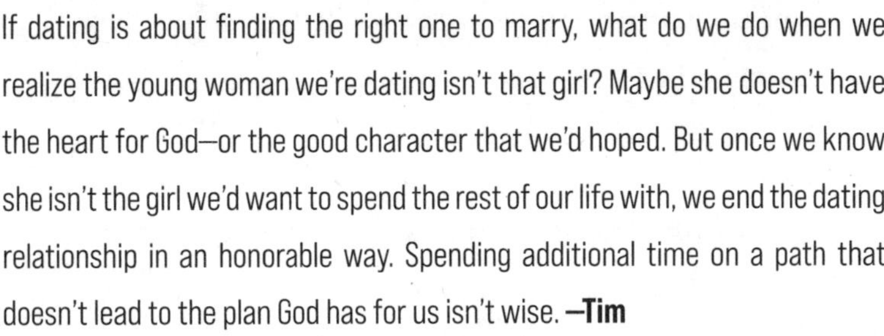

If dating is about finding the right one to marry, what do we do when we realize the young woman we're dating isn't that girl? Maybe she doesn't have the heart for God—or the good character that we'd hoped. But once we know she isn't the girl we'd want to spend the rest of our life with, we end the dating relationship in an honorable way. Spending additional time on a path that doesn't lead to the plan God has for us isn't wise. **—Tim**

2

What's So Bad About Dating Just for Fun?

It's easy to make dating about us, and what we want. God's vision sounds great, but really, so does ours. Ours is usually more fun, with things that are immediately enjoyable. Sure, God's plan has some fun elements within it, but the best stuff doesn't come till way down the road. The temptation is to start dating for our own reasons, instead of God's purposes.

The way I (Mark) see it, here are some common reasons guys date. See if any apply to you.

> ***To affirm their identity and build up their own self-confidence.*** They love what it says to others that an attractive girl has chosen them.

> ***To go far physically with a girl.*** Dating becomes about experiencing the pleasure that is supposed to be reserved for marriage.

To enhance their own quality of life. They avoid loneliness and gain a partner who will care about their needs. Maybe it's a rebound relationship, or just a distraction from life's struggles.

Just to have fun. It could be a summer fling or a vacation hookup. In either case, they're driven by their desire for fun in the moment and bucket list experiences.

I could go on, but I think you get the point. Each one of these cases trade what God was doing in Genesis when He created this male/female relationship for our own selfish reasons. Whenever we stray from God's plan, we're making a mistake.

When we're dating a girl to see if she'll be that one that we'll marry, it should be fun. But we don't date *just* for fun. See the difference? Dating the right girl *is* fun—and leads to the wonders of marriage. Dating just *for* fun—even though that girl isn't really a candidate for me to marry—leads to pain, regret, and loss. **—Tim**

3

What's So Wrong with Dating Someone Who Doesn't Love Jesus?

It's easy to fall in love. A sweet girl who looks at us with adoring eyes can be almost intoxicating. I've (Tim) seen so many guys stray from God's plan for dating because they were attracted to a girl who wasn't a committed believer. If we date a girl—knowing she isn't the right type to marry—we take a huge risk. We can end up falling in love, and love is blind, right? The more we grow to like the wrong girl, the less we'll see that she's wrong for us. If the girl isn't a dedicated follower of Christ . . . if she isn't putting what she reads in the Bible into practice in her life? If you're not seeing the fruit of the Holy Spirit (love, joy, peace, patience, goodness, kindness, gentleness, self-control) evidenced—and increasing—in her life? Save yourself unspeakable pain and move on. Pronto!

Remember . . . *our enemy can use a girl's love for us as a lure to lead us away from God.* I've seen too many men fall for a woman who loves them—but isn't a wholehearted follower of Jesus. If they marry, life eventually becomes so much harder for those men. Without Jesus, she can't possibly be the helper God intended her to be. We must choose wisely. The girl you pursue will either strengthen your walk with the Lord or weaken it.

■ ■ ■

Mark: What about "missionary dating"? That's when a guy dates a girl who isn't saved, hoping she'll come to Christ. Here are a few reasons why we believe missionary dating is a bad idea:

> ***You'll likely change.*** Convictions get watered down, especially with how far to go physically. It's hard to stay focused on God when the person you're dating doesn't share the same convictions.
>
> ***It's not fair to who you're dating.*** You're basically saying, "I really like you, but in order for this to work long term, you need to change everything you live for."

It doesn't get easier to break up. The longer you're with her, the deeper your love will grow and the harder it'll be to break it off. If you don't stand by the conviction of God's vision for relationships at the start, it'll only get easier to compromise later.

■ ■ ■

Imagine yourself in a three-legged marathon, twenty-six miles over rugged ground. Every couple who finishes within a certain time period gets a million dollars! But if you miss the window of time, there's a $100k penalty. Now, as you're approaching the starting line, you're given a choice. You can be tied together facing the same direction, or with one facing backward and the other facing forward.

You'd both want to be going the same direction, for sure. The race will be tough enough to finish without one of you facing the opposite way.

This is a picture of marriage. It's like a marathon two-person, three-legged race. It won't always be easy. A million-dollar marriage is possible for any of us guys, but only if we're facing the same direction as our girl.

That's the fooler about dating someone who isn't dedicated to Jesus like you are. They can seem wonderful in every way. It makes us think we can overlook that one tiny issue of where they are spiritually. If we lace up in a three-legged race, we're just as close to the girl whether she's facing forward or backward. Our legs are touching either way we face, right?

But if the girl isn't a dedicated follower of Jesus, we can't *stay* close. "For those who live according to the flesh set their minds on the things of the flesh, but those who live according to the Spirit set their minds on the things of the Spirit" (Romans 8:5).

This girl, as wonderful as she may be, doesn't have the Holy Spirit like you do. She only has the flesh, and that won't be enough. That closeness you share right now can't last, according to the Bible. The Holy Spirit will be giving you new desires that your girlfriend—or eventually wife—won't share.

There will be conflict you can't foresee now. You'll argue about how often you go to church, how much money you give to the church, how to raise your kids, and so much more.

"For the desires of the flesh are against the Spirit, and the desires of the Spirit are against the flesh, for these are opposed to each other, to keep you from doing the things you want to do" (Galatians 5:17).

There will be conflict you can't foresee now. You'll chafe each other. There'll be times you're not at your best—and your wife will need the Holy Spirit to help her love you anyway. Without the Holy Spirit, she's left with only her feelings to guide her, and feelings change. You'll be going in opposite directions and end up fighting. You'll argue about how often you go to church, how much money you give to the church, how to raise your kids, and so much more. That will never get you that million-dollar marriage you desire. You'll have the Holy Spirit working in you to grow your love, joy, peace, gentleness, self-control, kindness, and patience—all of which are essential to a really good marriage. She won't have the Holy Spirit's help at all. The flesh will pull her toward selfishness, envy, anger, and worse. See how important it is to date a girl who is really dedicated to Jesus and who is following the leading of the Holy Spirit in her life?

When considering a girl to date, set the bar higher. If we're satisfied simply hearing that the girl we want to date is a Christian, we could be settling for much less than we could have. Think about adult Christians you know. Some are mean. Angry. Vindictive. Gossips. Proud. Selfish. Critical. Complainers. Grudge-holders. Hotheads. Hypocrites. Divisive. Envious. And yet, they claim to be followers of Christ.

We don't want to date someone who simply *claims* to love and follow Jesus. You want someone who is actually living that out.

Just because a girl says she goes to church, or believes in Jesus, or posts a Bible verse or a picture of herself reading her Bible with a candle and her mug, doesn't mean she is solid in her faith. You need to do more than just date someone who claims Christianity as a title or has loose evidence of it in her life. Her being "saved" is not a box to check, but a room to explore. We're looking to see how skillfully and consistently she's applying the Bible and living a gospel-focused life. **—Mark**

It was my senior year in high school. There were lots of girls who were my friends in our church youth group—but I hadn't dated much. I didn't have to. None of them really had the kind of heart that I'd hoped for in the girl I would marry someday.

Except one. Her name was Cheryl. I'd never met another girl who had a heart for God and living out His Word like she did. She was kind. Genuinely cared for others. And she was also a great listener. I could tell her anything—and I knew she wouldn't be telling the other girls about our conversations.

I told a friend that I'd been thinking about dating Cheryl. Immediately, he tried talking me out of it.

"Cheryl's not the kind of girl you *date*." He looked at me like I'd lost my mind. "She's the kind of girl you *marry*."

He'd missed what dating was supposed to be about. But he was right about one thing. She was the kind of girl who would make a great Christian wife. So, I took Cheryl out, despite his advice. Eventually I fell in love with her—and have a million-dollar marriage with her today.

Men, look for the girl who has that heart for God like you've never seen before. One who loves Jesus. One who actively puts what she reads in the Bible into practice. Go after that girl, and you've taken the first step toward a million-dollar marriage yourself.

4

How Far Can We Go Physically . . . What Would You Say Is Okay?

Let's start with several questions that will help you discover the answer to that, and then I'll (Tim) share our convictions.

> **Do you want to play it safe?** If you truly want to keep from messing up this relationship, you'll draw the line in a different spot than many of your friends. If you're just looking to see how far you can go and get away with it? You're already headed for trouble.

Do you understand who this girl's Father is? If she's a believer, her Father is Almighty God. You'll answer to *Him* for how you treat her, how well you protect her, and for how well you keep her from doing something that God calls sin.

Do you want to risk losing this girl? If the girl you're dating is the type you'd marry, pushing the limits physically may drive her to lose respect for you—or break up with you. You'll put her in a position where she believes she must choose between you and the Lord. If she chooses you, she didn't quite have the heart for God that you really want. If she chooses the Lord, you'll lose the girl who would've made a great wife.

Do you want to date this girl in a way that pleases God? Think really hard about this. A good woman is a gift from God. One of the conditions to this gift is that we don't "unwrap" this present . . . not until our wedding night.

Remember, the further you go with a girl, the more blind you'll be to who she really is (her true Christian character and level of dedication to Christ) and the more likely you'll mess things up.

If you want to play it safe, protect God's girl, date in a way that pleases God, and not risk losing the good woman God has put in your life? Only then are you ready to date.

You've probably already figured out the answer to the question, but here's our views on how far you can go:

- *Hold her hand, put your arm around her shoulder.* Other than that, keep your hands off her body. Breasts. Butt. Thighs. These are off limits, guys. The more you touch her, the more you'll *want* to touch her. And don't allow her to touch you in ways that will arouse you. Save it for the honeymoon. Good things come to those who wait.

- *Kissing . . . but with a word of caution.* I know some guys who didn't kiss a girl on the lips until they were engaged. For others, the first kiss on the lips was when they were pronounced husband and wife at their wedding ceremony. If you choose to kiss on the lips while dating, then I'm going to add a strong word of caution. Avoid passionate kissing. So, keep your mouth closed—and your tongue in your mouth. French kissing is a bad idea when you're dating. It fans the flames of passion, making it easier to mess up. Show some self-control, and it will pay off massively later.

This isn't allowing much . . . but it's enough. Does adopting these guidelines guarantee you'll never sin or be tempted to? No. That's more of a heart issue. But if your heart is to do this dating thing right—in a way that pleases God and protects your girl—setting up some personal safeguards is wise. You'll also get to know her better if you keep things less physical, and that's a good thing. It will honor your Father, and hers. It will cause her to love and respect you more. It will help keep you from being blinded and making bad decisions. Sounds like a pretty good way to date, don't you think?

The Bible tells us to run from youthful lusts. Don't unwrap God's gift to you until the time when He says it's okay to do that . . . and that time is after you've married her.

One last word of caution here. "Sex" has been redefined by our culture, and by many in the church. Some will want you to believe that having oral sex isn't sex. That's ridiculous. If the word "sex" is in the name, of course it's sex! Some Christians say it's okay to sleep together before you're married. That's insanity. That is not at all what the Bible says.

> It is God's will that you should be sanctified: that you should avoid sexual immorality; that each of you should learn to control your own body in a way that is holy and honorable, not in passionate lust like the pagans, who do not know God; and that in this matter no one should wrong or take advantage of a brother or sister. The Lord will punish all those who commit such sins, as we told you and warned you before.
> (1 Thessalonians 4:3–6 NIV)

> But sexual immorality and all impurity or covetousness must not even be named among you, as is proper among saints. (Ephesians 5:3)

> Now the works of the flesh are evident: sexual immorality, impurity, sensuality, idolatry, sorcery, enmity, strife, jealousy, fits of

> anger, rivalries, dissensions, divisions, envy, drunkenness, orgies, and things like these. I warn you, as I warned you before, that those who do such things will not inherit the kingdom of God. (Galatians 5:19–21)

Don't compromise because you listened to someone who twisted God's words. Be wise. God doesn't change. His Word doesn't change. And He doesn't wink at sin. Would you do any of those things if her dad were in the room watching? Of course not. But her heavenly Father is always watching; and when you take a girl out, you're to be her protector. You're not to take advantage of her in any way. Trust God enough to do it His way. Love God enough to obey Him.

Marriage will come sooner than you imagine. Choose to guard yourself—and your date—by dating God's way. You'll enjoy the gift of intimacy in your marriage without any regrets.

5

Some Say a Guy Should Lead Spiritually, While Others Say I Should Find a Girl Who Challenges Me to Grow. Which Is It?

It's both. Guys, we should lead the charge when it comes to spiritual things. But men, let me (Tim) encourage you; we also want a girl who'll encourage us to be everything God has created us to be.

Here's a list of some ways any guy can lead spiritually, no matter his personality, comfort zone, or leadership style.

- Don't push the physical boundaries when on a date. We don't want to rely on our girl to put the brakes on things if we're going too far physically. We must lead.

- Have your personal time with God daily. And put what you learn into practice. The kind of Christian girl you really want will be looking for this in a man.

- Talk to your date about spiritual things. What are you reading in the Bible now? Have conversations with her about that. See where she lines up on those issues.

- Initiate getting to church—and serving there. If we rely more on her for this area, she won't respect that, which means she won't respect us.

- When you're at church and the worship band is playing—sing your heart out, even if you can't sing well. It's a way you can lead.

- Take notes during the sermon. If we don't take notes, we're saying, "I know I won't remember as much as I would if I *did* take notes, but I'm okay with that." A girl with a heart for God won't be impressed. So, let's take notes, and initiate talking with her afterward about the truth shared in the sermon.

- Watch how you're treating her parents—and yours. God promises to bless those who honor parents.

You might ask, if I'm looking for a girl who challenges me to grow, doesn't that suggest she's taking the lead spiritually?

Not at all. We absolutely want a girl who desires us to be the Christian man we should be and who finds that attractive. My wife has always had that effect on me, from way back when we were dating. Even now, I work at it, and often ask God to help me be the man she believes I am.

Is There Really Only One "Right" Person for Me?

You've probably heard the saying, "There are plenty of fish in the sea." I've (Mark) usually heard that spoken to someone who just had a hard breakup, or who really *needs* to break up. It's how we tell someone, "Hey, there are so many more options out there. You need to do a little more fishing!"

But the question is this. Are we choosing a girl like a kid picks a fish at the pet store? *I really like this one!* Or does God have one specifically picked out for us and we have no say in the matter? Kind of like a fisherman . . . we cast out the line and get what we get?

You'll get different answers depending on who you ask. A lot of this is open to interpretation of how God's will works. With that in mind, let's start with what we know, and work our way from there.

There is such a thing as the "wrong one" for you. Actually, there are a lot of girls who fall into that category, starting with any girl who is not a follower of Jesus. We already covered that extensively. We don't need to wonder if it's His will for us to marry someone who doesn't love and follow God. It's not. He's already made that clear in the Bible.

So, does that mean every single believing girl on the planet is a potential spouse? Can we really pick any Christian girl to marry, and still be in line with the will of God? I think we can all answer this question based on what we've observed and experienced. Is every Christian girl you've met someone you could see yourself marrying? Easy answer: No. We've met girls who love God, but we'd never be interested in a relationship with them, for a lot of legit reasons.

Over the course of your life (especially high school and college), there'll be a lot of Christian girls you're attracted to for different reasons. Their looks. Their personality. Their character. The way they follow Jesus. How do we know if they're the one?

Yes, we're fishing in a smaller pond—and narrowed our list of potential mates by committing to only date Christian girls who love Jesus. But we're still left with the question . . . does God have one picked out for us?

It's here I want to shift the conversation a bit. Instead of trying to figure out if God has "just one" picked out for you, I'd rather focus on how to choose your "one" well. The goal is to choose one girl that you'll be with the rest of your life. If you choose well, she'll be a blessing in your life in such a way that you'll feel as though no other woman could have ever been the "right one." I can't imagine any other woman being able to sharpen/encourage/help me in the way that my wife, Sarah, does—or be able to be the friend/mom/love of my life that Sarah is. Is that because God chose her to be mine? It sure feels like it!

So how do you "choose your one" well? A lot of it will go back to the Foundational Five. Think through each of them for a second. Each of them helps you date well . . . and *choose* well. Focus on God's purpose for you. Exercise self-control. Be led by the Holy Spirit. Grow in your closeness with Jesus. Let the Bible be your guide—and put it into practice.

As you strengthen yourself in each of these areas, you gain wisdom and clarity that helps you see the kind of person you want to spend the rest of your life with. So often, I've seen guys focus on other things. Their physique. Landing that next date. Making their girlfriend so happy that they win her over. None of those will help those young men make a wise choice.

Instead, build the habit of living out the principles from the Foundational Five. Build these habits well, and watch how that helps you choose well who you date and how you date. Do that, and you'll put yourself in a perfect position to find your one.

▪ ▪ ▪

Tim: I'm guessing that some of you may be thinking, ***What if I believe I'm supposed to stay single?*** Do you believe God wants you to be single—at least for now—so that you can serve Him better or dedicate yourself to the plan you believe He has for you? That can be a good thing, and there's value in that. Here's something the apostle Paul said:

"To the unmarried and the widows I say that it is good for them to remain single, as I am. But if they cannot exercise self-control, they should marry. For it is better to marry than to burn with passion" (1 Corinthians 7:8–9).

If you're single right now, you're not *less*. God has great purpose for you right where you are. And if you're single, but you desire marriage, that singleness may change. Bring it to God.

"He who finds a wife finds a good thing and obtains favor from the Lord" (Proverbs 18:22).

He who ***finds*** . . . I like the way that verse opens. This verse reminds us that we may have to do some searching. A good wife is a gift from God. A treasure, and treasure-hunting isn't always easy and it definitely takes some time. So, ask God to be your guide, and trust His timing.

Ask God to help you fall in love with the heart of the girl who'll make a great mate. Were there a number of girls I could've fallen in love with? Sure. But I wanted God to pick the one who would be best for me. And I definitely wanted God to make me worthy of that girl. He's the one who truly knows my heart, and the heart of the girl who'd make a great wife for me. He's the one who would know exactly how to help make me into a great husband for her. I asked Him to lead me to the one He'd pick to be *my* one. That prayer worked out really well!

7

Dating Seems to Come Easy for Some Guys. Am I the Only One Who Feels Really Awkward on a Date?

Short answer? No. Deep down we all feel awkward in some way. I (Mark) remember writing a song about one of my first crushes, and the whole song was about how awkward I was when I was around her. Did I ever work up the guts to play her the song? No way, that would have been *way* too awkward.

Can we overcome this?

I'm convinced that a lot of it is internal. It's this running dialogue in your head full of self-critique and comparison. We set an expectation for every interaction with this girl to be perfect. Smooth. Winsome. Not only are these standards unreachable, but it's an unrealistic way to build a relationship. It's not real life, and maybe more importantly, that's not how we're supposed to "win the girl."

So, take a quick check of your expectations on yourself. Are you evaluating every single interaction? Dissecting your witty comments and rating how hard she laughed? Good news, you can stop all of that. It matters way less than we think.

Another way we get caught up in the awkwardness is when we work hard to look better than who we really are. False advertising at its finest! Which means, we actually aren't being ourselves. No wonder we feel awkward as we try to be someone who we weren't just five minutes before the date. We're much better off giving a full and fair representation of who we are, even with the quirks and awkward moments.

In other words, stop pretending to be someone you're not. Let her see who you are and fall in love with that guy. I'm telling you—you don't want her to fall in love with the fake you.

■ ■ ■

Tim: I love what Mark just said there! Put your best foot forward, sure. Clean up for the date. Wear a fresh set of clothes. Often the right girl will drive us guys to work at being better than we are in some ways, and that's all healthy. But to simply *cover* who we are—or *pretend* to be someone we're not? That'll destroy the trust with her that we want to build. We're headed for disaster.

■ ■ ■

Okay, last thing. And maybe the most important. Focus on the friendship. I (Mark) think we get awkward sometimes because we feel the pressure of dating. We work so hard trying to convince this person to like us and to be attracted to us. Instead, work on building a friendship, just like you've done with other people over the course of your life. Ask good questions. Show interest in her life. Find common interests. Have some fun. Find out where she is spiritually. See if you two can get to be better friends. Maybe you will. Great! And if she doesn't have the same level of interest in you that you have in her, it's not time to blame your awkwardness. It's just that you're one of the billions of other guys she's not going to marry.

8

What Does It Look Like to Date with God's Vision in Mind?

A good starting place is to ask yourself: *Would God be pleased with who I'm taking out, how I've prepared for the date, and how we spend our time together on the date itself?*

With that in mind, here are some reminders I (Tim) think you'd want to review.

> ***Remember the purpose for dating.*** To find the one you believe you're to marry.

Commit to follow God's guidelines for how far you go physically. How can you keep yourself from being tempted? Make a list. Things like . . .

> *Don't sit in the car alone with her to talk.* Go someplace public . . . not so secluded.
>
> *Don't spend time alone with her at her home, dorm, apartment—or yours.* You're asking for trouble.

Pray before you meet her for the date. Ask God to help you be the man you should be when you're with her. Ask Him to help you encourage her be the girl He wants her to be. Ask Him to show you if she's the one for you.

Spend time talking. If you're watching a movie or playing a video game, it's hard to get to know the girl. Not that you can't do those things, just be sure you're leaving enough time for conversation. If one or the other of you is showing phone addiction signs, that needs to be considered or talked about. And talk about everything . . . your views on spiritual things . . . and life. Is this the kind of person you'd like to spend the rest of your life with?

Dating is a treasure hunt, not a pleasure hunt.

Get to know her family. If you marry this girl, her family will always be part of *your* family. Make sure that will work. Treat them the way you'd like to be treated, and you'll be building a relationship with them too.

Get wise counsel. Talk to others who have a marriage that you respect. Ask them for their thoughts on what's important when dating.

Be honest. Nothing turns a girl off quicker than a guy who pretends to be someone he isn't. Instead of using our energy to hide who we are, put our efforts into becoming the man, with God's help, that He's designed you to be.

Have fun. It's okay to have fun on a date. If this girl is looking more and more like the kind you would marry, it's pretty important that you can have fun together.

Guys, dating is a treasure hunt, not a pleasure hunt. If we really seek out the kind of girl who loves God with all her heart and lives that out? We'll find treasure—and plenty of pleasure after marriage as well. If we jump into dating for the selfish thrills it may bring now, likely we'll experience a ton of pain and miss God's best . . . the treasure He has for us.

■ ■ ■

Mark: People LOVE . . . *love*. Whether they're a follower of Jesus or not, we love relationships. Have you ever been in a stadium when the song "Sweet Caroline" comes on? The excitement in the arena as everyone sings along with the words "hands . . . touching hands." You can't help but smile as you belt out "Sweet Caroline . . . BAH-BAH-BAH." For that moment, we all agree that love is the best.

God gave us something so amazing when He created love. To experience it to the fullest, we should pursue love as God intended it to be from the start.

▪ ▪ ▪

Everything God created is good. And marriage can be so good. Dating with God's vision in mind is a step in that direction. His vision for marriage is totally worth pursuing.

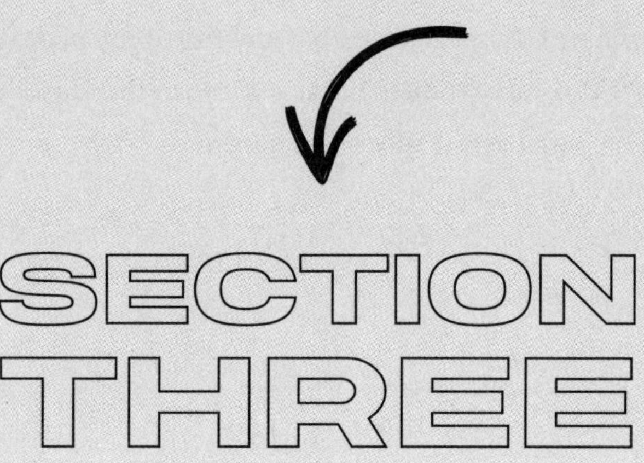
SECTION
THREE

DECISIONS

I (Mark) rely on Google Maps more than I need to, especially on a long road trip. I keep the map on, checking it every so often to see if I've shaved any minutes off the arrival time.

Recently, I was with a bunch of college students making the twelve-hour drive home from a conference. Suddenly, Google maps suggested a new, *faster* route, which meant taking the exit only a mile ahead. We had to make a decision, and *quick*.

I didn't check the route this shortcut would lead us on; all I cared about was getting home at 1:00 a.m. instead of 1:45 a.m.—so we took the exit. I liked the new arrival time, but honestly? I had some nagging uncertainty about our decision to change course. Was it even possible to save that much time?

Minutes after exiting, we saw brake lights ahead. Traffic came to a stop, and the arrival time got later and later. I grabbed my phone and looked more carefully at this new route. Lots of two-lane country roads through small towns. Lots of turns. All of it unfamiliar to me, and we'd be driving it late at night. I quickly checked our previous course, and to my shock, now Google showed our original route to be the faster by a solid thirty minutes.

I was flooded with regret. Why had I changed course? What a stupid decision! Now I—and the students—had to live with the consequences of that one decision for the next six hours of the drive.

You have decisions ahead. Will I go to college, and if so, which one? What will my major be? What will I do for a living? Which internship should I take? Should I date that person? Are we ready to get engaged? Who are my real friends? Is that job right for me? Where will I live? Which church should I attend?

That's a lot of decisions. And each choice has ripple effects. Consequences—good or bad. That can feel overwhelming, right? The last thing we want is to make decisions that lead to delays, reroutes, and regret.

How can we make decisions that don't lead to regret? How can we make wise decisions when there are so many options? How do we make right decisions when they seem to come at us so fast?

Let's talk about some important decision-making principles to guide you on the road you're traveling.

How Do I Know if I'm Making the Right Decision?

Decisions can paralyze us—especially those big ones. Here are the five big things I (Tim) have learned over the years about making good decisions.

> ***Ask God to lead.*** The quicker we bring God into the process, the better. When we ask Him to guide us, why wouldn't He do that?
>
> ***Search the Word.*** Are there principles we need to be putting into practice? The answer may be obvious. And sometimes we need to take action on what we know we should be doing before we'll get more clarity on whatever bigger decision we're wrestling with.
>
> ***Get input from the wise and godly.*** I usually got my best advice from those who'd experienced more of life, not just my friends. People who were older and often already part of my life. Parents. Grandparents. Pastors. Or maybe a man at church who is strong in his walk with Christ. Take him out for coffee—and get some input.
>
> ***Trust the leading you've received.*** The principles you've seen in the Word. The direction you're sensing

deep in your heart. The wise counsel you've received. These should join together to lead us to a next step. Trust that God is leading through that process.

Move out. Once we sense His leading, we need to take action—even if I only know the next step. We have to get moving.

■ ■ ■

Sometimes the next step is a small one. I (Mark) remember a time in college when I was faced with a looming decision. As I talked to my dad about it, he asked me, "Do you have a next step?" Well, yeah, I did. I didn't have the big decision worked out yet, but I did have a next step, as small and insignificant as it seemed.

What often paralyzes us in decision-making is our inability to see every step we need to make—or how it will all turn out. It feels like we're taking a shot in the dark. We feel we don't have enough information.

Take the next step that you see, even when you don't know what the next three moves will be. As you walk forward, you'll have more clarity. In my life, God has consistently given direction through a bunch of little steps before making the one big decision. He often doesn't show us everything all at once. God wants us to exercise our faith. As we take the step that He's showing us now, He will continue to show you the next step . . . and the next. But we have to start with that small step that we know we should take.

■ ■ ■

Sometimes there isn't time to put all five of these into play. We have to make a decision—*fast*. This is where it really helps to know the Bible. The more you're in the Word, the more you'll be guided by its principles—and making great decisions. Even quick ones. I (Tim) also live by a simple personal rule. *When in doubt, don't.* Sometimes the need for a quick decision is about a purchase, or because someone is pressuring us. If I'm questioning the wisdom of that decision—and there isn't time to really think or pray about it—I've learned to say no.

■ ■ ■

Mark: Here's a good question to ask before making decisions. *How has my time with God been lately?* Psalm 37:4 says, "Delight yourself in the Lord, and he will give you the desires of your heart." The more time we spend with God (in His word, in prayer, enjoying time with Him), the more our desires and decisions will be in sync with His will.

■ ■ ■

There are times we don't get the decision right. When that happens, we have other decisions to make.

- Can I get a do-over to fix the bad choice? I don't want to keep going in the wrong direction simply because I dread the time, work, or embarrassment of going back.
- When there's no turning back, can I course-correct and move on? We don't want to waste time beating ourselves up.

- Sometimes a bad decision means making some apologies, too. Let's do the right thing.

■ ■ ■

Back to that road trip I (Mark) was talking about earlier: Once I realized the new route I'd chosen was a bad choice, part of me didn't want to take the time to turn around. But I didn't want to stay where I was either. I decided to take the next exit, and I made my way back to the route I'd started on.

We can always learn and grow from the mistakes we make. And sometimes, we can turn around and choose to get back on the path we know we should have been on all along.

10

Does God Care About the Small Decisions of Life?

Have you ever seen a photographic mosaic? That's when one large image is made up of many smaller pictures. The first one I (Mark) remember seeing was of Abraham Lincoln. At first glance, it just looked like a portrait of Lincoln. But as I looked closer, I saw there were hundreds of small, tiled images of Abe throughout his life within the image. All the small and less noticeable images came together to form one large and very distinct picture of Abraham Lincoln.

I think it's helpful to view our lifetime of decision-making as a photographic mosaic. Each of the small images represents a decision in our life. When you compile all of them together, they form one large picture of who we are and what our entire life is about.

The Bible shows us what the large portrait of our life should look like. When anyone steps back and looks at the sum of our life, they should see a lifetime of us choosing to follow God—just as Jesus taught. The big picture of our life should show that we faithfully love God—and others. For that to happen, it'll take thousands of decisions consistently reflecting that. When tiled all together, they'll reveal a mosaic of one who is becoming the man God designed him to be.

We can easily identify the big decisions in life. Sometimes smaller decisions feel less important, so we tend to give them less attention. We often make these decisions selfishly or without God in mind.

We can easily identify the big decisions in life. Because they impact so much, we give them a lot of attention. Who we marry, the career we pursue, the church we attend, and where we live—to name a few. We understand the importance of these decisions when it comes to forming the mosaic of our life, and we're usually pretty quick to pray about them, seeking God's guidance.

Sometimes smaller decisions feel less important, so we tend to give them less attention. We often make these decisions selfishly or without God in mind. But we can't forget, all these decisions are forming the bigger picture of who we are. Here are some examples of things that may seem more like small decisions to many. I'm sure you could add to this list.

- How much we spend on the stuff we wear and the stuff we use
- The way we use our free time

- Our work ethic on Friday afternoon
- The shows we watch
- How we treat our coworkers
- How we speak to clerks or employees we don't know
- Which friends we keep close
- What things we post or repost
- How we answer a text—or if we do
- Our tone of voice when we talk to or about others who annoy us
- Sometimes the types of food or amounts that we eat
- Whether or not we exercise
- Personal choices about alcohol (Is it okay for me? If so, are there limits as to how much? How often? Are there personal convictions that may limit if, when, where, or why to drink?)
- How consistent we are at going to church
- Whether or not we get involved to volunteer, serve, or attend a small group at church
- How much money we give to the church—and how often

■ ■ ■

Tim: Sometimes the small decisions matter more than we think they do. Living in a land with so many freedoms, we often think that we can do whatever we want with our free time or money—as if our decisions were totally up to us. We may think of God as the boss and ourselves as employees. An employee's workday ends. Once at home, employees don't answer to the boss. If we adopt the boss/employee mentality, there's a problem. We'll begin to act like there are times that we're not on the clock and are free to do whatever we choose to do with our time, because it's *my* time.

The truth? Jesus saved us from our own sin and from the death penalty we deserve. He paid our ransom. He *bought* us. We're not His employees. We're *His*. We belong to Him, like *servants*; and servants are only good and wise if they're consistently considering what's best for their master—even in the small decisions.

▪ ▪ ▪

I (Mark) started regularly praying Psalm 86:11 a while back. It says, "Teach me your way, O LORD, that I may walk in your truth; unite my heart to fear your name."

When we ask Him to teach us His way, it requires that we aim to please God in every decision, no matter how minor it seems. When we ask God to unite our heart to fear His name, it forces us to put all of who we are under submission to please Him. When our whole heart fears His name, we don't let any corner of our decision-making go rogue. We're committing to making a full mosaic of faithfulness to God.

It's important to point out that there are some decisions that don't lead to sin—no matter which option we choose. In those cases, we have that freedom to choose without worrying about how that will affect our faithfulness to God. Things like the color of your car, what you choose to eat for dinner tonight, where you go on vacation, which shoes you wear, or if you get your coffee from Dunkin' or Starbucks—although I do have a strong opinion on that!

But the fact that there are small decisions that matter to God helps reinforce how important it is that we continue to let the Holy Spirit control us. The more focus we put into being led by the Spirit, the more our decision-making reflex will be right, time after time, for those thousands of small, tiled pictures we're putting together into the complete mosaic.

■ ■ ■

Tim: Maybe you're thinking, *what if I've messed up too much?* Every Christian man I know has made countless bad decisions. That's where God's grace and forgiveness come in. In the Bible, Paul made some pretty bad decisions before he truly encountered Jesus. But he gratefully accepted His forgiveness—and didn't focus on his past.

"One thing I do: forgetting what lies behind and straining forward to what lies ahead, I press on toward the goal for the prize of the upward call of God in Christ Jesus" (Philippians 3:13b–14).

We can do the same. We ask Him to forgive us—fully trusting He will. And, if appropriate, we make apologies and restitution to others if our bad decisions have hurt them. Then, we ask God to help us not make bad decisions like that again. Now, we stop looking back and move on. Trust God to do good things in us and through us, even after we've made bad decisions.

I Can Trust Google to Navigate Me Around the World. Why Not Trust Google to Guide Me in Life Too?

The idea of a satellite pinpointing where my (Tim) vehicle is—and the most efficient way to get to my next destination? That's great. But when it comes direction for my life, I'm going to want to seek a source that's a *lot* higher than any satellite.

Using Google is like devouring fast-food—except in the information business. Google gives answers that fill the hole you've got for the moment. It provides quick answers, but you're missing some of the better and far more valuable benefits to seeking counsel from *others.*

Tutorial vs. tutor. Don't get me wrong, there's lots of great information we can get online. But it's like comparing a tutorial to an actual tutor. A tutorial is one-size-fits-all. A real live person's help is personalized to us. When I was learning to write, especially fiction, I learned exponentially more when I had someone mentoring me than I did any other way. It was a far better use of my time.

Many of my tutors have been for a season of life—and that's fine. But there are a few who've been mentors for years. One of the practical benefits to that is they get to know me, really well. They know my tendencies and weaknesses. As they speak into that, they help me make better and wiser decisions. **—Mark**

Relying on AI or going to a stranger rather than to someone we know. Let's face it, we don't really know who's behind the advice Google gives, or what agenda that represents. And we can be sure that Google has no idea of the plans God has for our life. How can Google guide us when it really doesn't know where we're supposed to go? When we choose to ask a real person for advice, we know where the input is coming from—and they know us too. If they know us well enough, they may already have a sense of God's direction for our life. Their advice becomes incredibly valuable! They'll likely pray for us too. We'll never get Google to do that!

Satellite solutions vs. spiritual solutions. We're quick to seek online solutions. Often, we don't even consider praying about it—or searching the Word—and as a result, we end up missing better and more complete answers.

So much about manhood comes down to the little things. The small things we do that make us stand out in some way. When we go to God and real people for direction, we end up picking up so many things that will round us out in ways Google never can.

12

How Can I Tell the Difference Between Good Advice and Not-So-Good Advice?

There are some powerful stories in the Bible of men who followed bad advice—and paid heavily for it. We can probably think of some personal or family examples too. But sometimes even bad advice sounds *good.* How can we tell the difference? Here's my (Tim) top five suggestions.

Consider the Word. Does every bit of the advice we're getting square with the Bible? I know a Christian man who followed someone's advice to do something the Bible clearly speaks against—in hopes of achieving a greater good. In justifying his decision, he said the part that conflicted with the Bible was just a "necessary evil." He got bad advice. Choosing to do evil is never necessary.

Consider the source. What do we really know about the person giving the advice? Are they careful to follow the whole Word in their personal life? Do we believe they have our best interests at heart, or do we sense there are other motives? Psalm 1 warns us against taking the advice of those who aren't walking with God.

Consider your experience. What has God taught you in the past through your own experience, or that of others you know? Run the advice through that filter.

Consider another opinion. Is there a second, trusted source you can consult to verify the advice you're getting is good or not? Someone who knows you—and the Word. Someone you consider to be wise.

Consider talking to God about it more than you already have. Bringing the advice before God and asking Him to lead and guide? That's a good decision right there. Trust that He'll make it clear to you.

> "Trust in the LORD with all your heart, and do not lean on your own understanding. In all your ways acknowledge him, and he will make straight your paths" (Proverbs 3:5–6).

Following good advice can save us time, money, embarrassment, and all sorts of regret. A man who seeks wise advice—and actually takes that counsel—is well on his way to becoming wise himself.

When Is Stalling on a Decision Good vs. When Is It Wrong?

I want you to imagine this scenario with me (Mark). You're on your way to work, waiting at a red light. The light turns green, but the car in front of you doesn't move. The driver's head is down—looking at their phone. *Great. They're distracted. Probably picking out their next song or seeing what's new on Instagram since they checked at the last light.*

How long do you wait before honking? There's something inside us that hates sitting at a green light instead of moving forward. It just feels wrong. Our instinct tells us to DRIVE!

There's a growing trend of a similar kind of stalling in decision-making. Guys are sitting at green lights, so to speak. Instead of moving forward when they should, they wait. This approach has gotten confused with wisdom and maturity. I've seen guys miss out on green lights and good things God had for them, all because they stalled off a decision to move forward. I've watched guys squander years of their life and amazing opportunities, all because they chose to keep their foot on the brake when they should've been hitting the gas.

What are examples of a green light—a clear signal to move forward with a decision? I'm so glad you asked.

God's Word clearly teaches what decision to make. At this point it's a matter of obedience to move forward.

Solid Christian friends, mentors, and leaders affirm the decision.

After praying about it, you sense God's leading toward an opportunity.

You have a clear idea of the next step you should take after asking God to lead you.

The Bible often makes green and red lights clear. *Should I really forgive that person who wronged me?* Yes. *Should I really break off a relationship with a girl who doesn't follow Jesus?* Yes. The Bible gives green lights for those decisions. If I stall on things like those, that would be wrong, and likely I'll hear some horns honking from solid Christian friends, mentors, or parents. **—Tim**

But we get so comfortable at certain intersections, don't we? The next part of our journey intimidates us. We become fearful of what the future holds. All the unknowns. We don't want the added responsibility that comes with driving farther up the road. We don't want change. So, we sit at a green, and hope no one honks.

And just like the driver ahead of us on their phone, we find distractions as we sit there, going nowhere. Sometimes it's a relationship, job, video games, or hobbies. We immerse ourselves in all sorts of things so we don't have to pay attention to the green light and the responsibility on us to drive forward. You might have friends who are sitting at the green light. That doesn't mean it's okay for you to do that also.

These friends are stalling instead of taking action on what they really should be doing. Don't follow their lead. Look in a mirror, my friend. That's a man you're seeing. And as a man, God has things He's planned for you to do.

"When I was a child, I spoke like a child, I thought like a child, I reasoned like a child. When I became a man, I gave up childish ways" (1 Corinthians 13:11).

You have the green light to focus your energies into becoming the man God designed you to be so you can do the things He's planned for you to do. You have the green light to serve Him like you never did before. Often, we've been given all God knows we need to move forward. It's on us to take our foot off the brake and hit the accelerator. It's not a matter of when *we* feel ready. We've been told to go. If we don't drive, we're choosing to stay stuck in a place that isn't our destination. Which means we aren't just stalling. We're disobeying.

There'll be times you have a clear red light in decision-making. You should follow that signal and wait before pressing ahead.

That isn't stalling. It's not irresponsibility or laziness either. It's actually the wisest way to navigate your situation. Here are some examples:

> You haven't prayed about it or looked in God's Word for guidance.
>
> You haven't talked to a mentor or church leader about it.
>
> Or you *have* talked to a mentor, and they express concern about the decision you're making.
>
> You haven't done real digging to get all the information you need to make a wise decision.
>
> Through one or more of the above, you're sensing God doesn't want you to move forward yet.

These are all red lights. Valid reasons to wait before proceeding. Even though you'd love to put this decision in your rearview mirror, you're actually navigating this road well by waiting for God to give you the green light.

Let's be the kind of men who know when to wisely wait at the red light, and how to quickly move forward when it turns green. When we do that, we'll find ourselves on the roads that lead us into God's great purposes for our life.

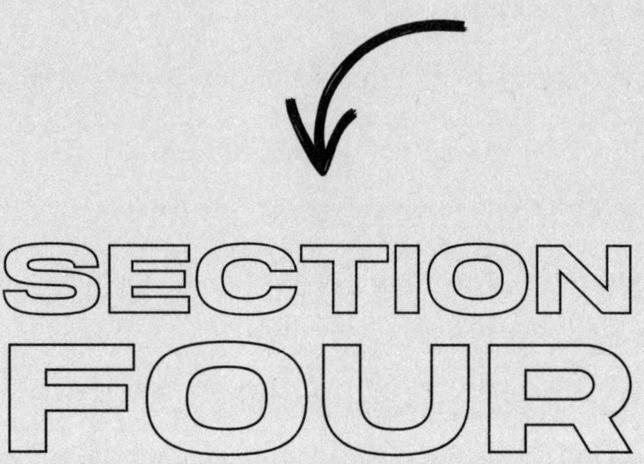
SECTION
FOUR

HARD EMOTIONS

One of my (Tim) favorite stories of David, the man who would later become king of Israel, describes his darkest hour. A time of fear, anxiety, anger, and massive grief. David's reaction to this tempest of emotions locked his men's loyalty to him for life. He put into practice a technique he'd learned earlier—and now it stopped an angry mob bent on killing him. It saved the lives of plenty of others too.

In 1 Samuel 30, David, his six hundred men, and their families lived in Ziklag. David had allied himself to Achish, the Philistine king, in a bold move to stay safe from Israel's jealous King Saul.

Eventually, Achish invited David and his army to fight alongside him against the Israelites. But after a three-day march to the battle lines, the commanders under King Achish insisted that David and his men leave. They didn't trust David, and feared he'd turn against them in battle. It was a humiliating moment for David's band of fighters.

Angry and discouraged, David and his men returned to Ziklag, only to find the town had been burned and looted by a raiding Amalekite army. Their wives and kids . . . all of them had been taken captive.

Now it wasn't only anger and discouragement that overwhelmed the men. Lethal doses of fear were added. And grief. Hopelessness. Despair. Anxiety. David and his men wept until they had no strength to weep anymore. Bitterness seeped through them to their very core. And then the unthinkable happened. Looking for someone to blame, David's men—including his own family—turned on him. He was surrounded, with no chance of escape. David's men were trained killers, and they wanted to kill *him*.

Then David does something that changed *everything*.

"David strengthened himself in the Lord his God" (1 Samuel 30:6b).

Strengthening ourselves in the Lord . . . what does that even mean? Let's not make it harder or more mysterious than it is.

Strengthening ourselves in the Lord is about remembering . . .

who God is (e.g., all powerful)

what God is like (e.g., loving, compassionate)

what God has done historically (e.g., Bible stories, family history)

what God has done for me (times He's helped me, bailed me out)

how He loves me and will never abandon me

how He's in control, and in the end, we win

key Bible verses we've memorized

that we can go to Him with anything at any time, knowing He hears and cares.

All this and more is how we strengthen ourselves in the Lord. As we practice, we'll get better—and quicker at it. This practice of strengthening ourselves like this totally bolsters our faith. David had done this before—over and over in the book of Psalms and once while with his good friend Jonathan. That practice paid off, because David had to do it quickly here.

David was battered with some of the hardest emotions a man can face, and all at the same time. That quick ability to strengthen himself in the Lord gave David the clarity of mind and faith to take the next step—seek direction from God—even while surrounded by a murderous mob. "LORD, shall I pursue after this band?" (30:8).

David was convinced God was leading him to chase down that raiding army. Once again, David took the next step without any delay. His men saw this surge of strength and leadership in

How will our life be different—and better—if we learn to strengthen ourselves in the Lord?

David, and instead of killing him, they followed him on one of the greatest rescue missions of all time. In the end, David and his exhausted little army saved every last woman and child. It's a fantastic story.

How about *our* story? Yours. Mine. How will our life be different—and better—if we learn to strengthen ourselves in the Lord? In a clutch situation, we'll need to strengthen ourselves in the Lord *fast,* as David did. That means we need to practice strengthening ourselves so that we can do it quickly. So that it comes naturally. A great time to do that? When we wake up in the morning. Before you swing your legs out of bed, run down that list of things that we know about God. Do that day after day, and you'll build a habit.

Now, when we're surrounded by hard emotions, we'll be able to put that strengthening technique into motion quickly. That'll get our eyes off ourselves and onto Him. It'll strengthen our faith. Now, with our boosted faith, we go to the Lord for direction. What if, once we had an idea of our next step, we took it—even though we didn't know the step after that? What if we moved forward, trusting God would lead us . . . one step at a time? How might our story be different when hard emotions seem to have us surrounded, with no hope of escape? I can guess what David would say. *It would mean the difference between life—and death.*

It Seems Everybody Wrestles with Some Level of Anxiety. Isn't It Something I Just Need to Live With?

I (Mark) wish you could see the spot where I'm writing this. I have the perfect window seat at a busy coffee shop in the heart of the city, overlooking the Chicago River, surrounded by skyscrapers and crowds of people.

Everyone around me has places to be, deals to make, and deadlines to meet. The guy next to me stares at a screen of charts with red arrows going down. The guy outside my window paces back and forth while taking a call. And then there's me, trying to get some writing done before I catch the 4:05 train out of the city.

It feels a bit ironic to be writing about anxiety in a place where I am surrounded by it. But really, who isn't surrounded by it these days? Our culture talks about managing our anxiety, coping with it, or just plain suffering through it. Notice, every option attempts to reduce anxiety at best, without ever offering a way to be truly free from it.

The fact is there's a solution.

God gives us two major truths that I believe are the antidote for anxiety. God also gives us something we can do every day that helps remove anxiety. Two truths and a technique to try. (Sorta sounds like we're about to play a new rendition of "two truths and a lie.")

In Matthew 6:25 Jesus says, "Therefore I tell you, do not be anxious about your life."

Okay, so, just don't be anxious? *That's* the solution?

Wait, keep reading.

"Look at the birds of the air: they neither sow nor reap nor gather into barns, and yet your heavenly Father feeds them. Are you not of more value than they?" (v. 26).

***Truth #1:* Remember, if God takes care of the birds, He'll take care of us.**

The things I get anxious about are the things in the future I can't control. We get anxious about relationships, the job or internship we hope to get, the bills that just keep stacking up . . . as if it's all on us.

Jesus says, *Good news! I control all of that. And if I take care of the birds, doesn't that mean I'll take even better care of you?*

I actually did this right now, from the coffee shop. The first bird I spotted out that downtown Chicago window was a pigeon. As I stared at that nasty, ragged pigeon, surviving off the scraps of the city, the point Jesus was getting at struck me.

God provides for this pigeon, and I'm more valuable to God than this pigeon. So why would I be anxious about the things in my future I can't control? He'll take care of me. That truth speaks right to the heart of some of my deepest anxieties.

Okay, time for our second truth.

***Truth #2:* God's Spirit inside us produces the peace of God in our heart.**

Once we put our faith in Jesus, God puts His Spirit within us, which is a big deal when it comes to anxiety. Galatians 5 lists supernatural effects of having the Spirit in our life. There's love, joy, and *peace*. That level of peace doesn't come from coping mechanisms or finding distractions, but from the presence of God within us this very moment. The power of His Spirit gives us hope to overcome any anxiety.

A technique to try: Pray through your anxiety.

"Do not be anxious about anything, but in everything by prayer and supplication with thanksgiving let your requests be made known to God. And the peace of God, which surpasses all understanding, will guard your hearts and your minds in Christ Jesus" (Philippians 4:6–7).

When we bring our anxiety to God, He helps us surrender the things we're trying to control. As we pray, God helps us trust His sovereign plan and the care He has for our lives. When's the last time you prayed and truly believed God could give you peace in the midst of that anxiety you face?

Sometimes the anxiety won't let go—or returns minutes later. When that happens, I repeat the process until I'm strengthened in the Lord and the peace sticks. And there are times when a man wrestling with hard emotions may need to seek the help of a professional therapist/psychologist who is a solid Christian. There's no shame in a man seeking help to fight free from emotions that have an iron grip on him. **—Tim**

I took one more look out the window before running to catch my train. Across the river sat a couple dozen lawn chairs on a patch of green grass. All the chairs were empty, except one. There, in the middle of the hustle and bustle of Chicago, sat a man. He looked so relaxed. Peaceful. A perfect visual of what we as believers can be. At rest, full of peace, even when anxiety is all around us.

Life Has Me Really Discouraged. Is There a Way Out of That— Short of a New Life?

Discouragement is more than some random emotion that sweeps over me (Tim) and you. It's an ancient, strategic weapon that our enemy uses for one reason. To defeat us.

Discouragement whispers to us . . .

Your situation is impossible—there's no fix for this.

This won't get better—it's too far gone.

This is more than you can handle—you'll absolutely fail.

Be afraid—the worst is yet to come.

There's no hope. Give up—throw in the towel; quit.

In the Old Testament book of Ezra, Israelites returning to Jerusalem began rebuilding the temple after years and years of being exiled to faraway places.

Enemies in surrounding lands didn't want the temple to be rebuilt. They didn't want the Israelites making efforts to reconnect to the Almighty God. So, they came up with a plan to use a very effective weapon. Discouragement.

"Then the people of the land discouraged the people of Judah and made them afraid to build" (Ezra 4:4).

We often take the wrong courses of action to beat discouragement. We look for escapes. Maybe something fun and exciting. Go out with friends. Take a trip. Change jobs. Change geography. Take on a new challenge. Learn a new skill. Go back to school. We think those types of things will chase away discouragement. Sure, they can help; but not enough, and not for long.

Let's recognize discouragement for what it often is for us as Christian men: an attack. A scheme of our enemies, the devil and his demons. They want us to lose our courage to move forward in the direction God has for us. If we don't recognize that discouragement as an attack, we'll look to fix our discouragement in ways that do us no good in the long run.

Because discouragement is often a spiritual weapon used against us, we must fight back using *our* spiritual weapons. Earlier in this section we talked about how David strengthened himself in the Lord. That list of things David did describes the practice of putting on our spiritual armor, doesn't it?

> Finally, be strong in the Lord and in the strength of his might. Put on the whole armor of God, that you may be able to stand against the schemes of the devil. For we do not wrestle against flesh and blood, but against the rulers, against the authorities, against the cosmic powers over this present darkness, against the spiritual forces of evil in the heavenly places. Therefore take up the whole armor of God, that you may be able to withstand in the evil day, and having done all, to stand firm.
> (Ephesians 6:10–13)

Once we understand the enemy is hitting us with discouragement because he's worried that we're on the right track and he's afraid we'll accomplish God's plans for us? That should in turn make us attack that flaming dart of discouragement with the faith that comes from strengthening ourselves in the Lord.

"In all circumstances take up the shield of faith, with which you can extinguish all the flaming darts of the evil one" (Ephesians 6:16).

Sometimes we don't see light at the end of the tunnel. Here's a favorite verse I cling to in those times: "Light dawns in the darkness for the upright; he is gracious, merciful, and righteous" (Psalm 112:4).

Discouraged? Strengthen yourself in the Lord. Fight discouragement with faith in our God who loves us. When all looks lost, and hope is nowhere to be found. When there is no light at the end of the tunnel . . . God has a way of bringing light into our life that we don't see coming.

■ ■ ■

I (Mark) can't count the number of times I've been riding high after some big spiritual moment and my mom has looked into my eyes and warned me that Satan will soon try to discourage me. Some of my darkest moments of discouragement have come after a great spiritual victory. Those talks from my mom taught me that we should expect discouragement to come our way when we feel farthest from it. We know the play our enemy is going to run against us, so we should prepare for it and put up a solid defense against it.

16
Can I Beat Fear?

Like discouragement, fear is another ancient weapon used by our enemy. In the book of Nehemiah, the Israelites in Jerusalem began rebuilding the protective wall surrounding their city. It had been destroyed generations before, and now God led Nehemiah to rally the people to undertake the daunting project.

Enemies living nearby didn't want to see that happen any more than they'd wanted the temple rebuilt. They didn't attack the Israelites with spears or swords or arrows—although they wanted to. They used a more subtle, but effective weapon. Fear. But Nehemiah fought back, reminding the people of their great God. He strengthened them in the Lord.

> And I looked and arose and said to the nobles and to the officials and to the rest of the people, "Do not be afraid of them. Remember the Lord, who is great and awesome, and fight for your brothers, your sons, your daughters, your wives, and your homes." (Nehemiah 4:14)

When fear grips me (Tim), the most effective way I've found to fight it off is by strengthening myself in the Lord. This is our Kevlar vest as men. Nehemiah reminded them why it was so important to fight past the fear. It was about the protection of those they loved.

When you fight back against fear, you're fighting for your future.

The plans God has for you.

The wife and kids that you may have one day.

If you don't fight the effects of fear now, the enemy will derail you. If that happens, you won't experience all God has for you in the future.

I fought an eleven-month battle with various work and health fears. I don't think I realized at the time just how much of it was a spiritual attack, and I definitely didn't comprehend how tightly fear gripped me. I'd also planned a solo mission trip to Mexico, but now the whole idea seemed crazy. There were kidnappings going on in the area—and I was going down there alone? The enemy added more fear to what I was already harboring. I had a chance to back out but didn't think that was what God wanted for me. So, I took that next step that I believed God wanted me to take. I was still afraid but went to Mexico anyway. God did something amazing when I took that next fearful step. He rescued me from all my fears on that mission trip, and in His great mercy, He's kept that kind of fear from ever getting a toehold in my life since.

Fear has nuclear weapon power in a spiritual sense. It can stop us like nothing else can. Let's not let fear short-circuit God's plans for us.

- Fight back against fear by strengthening yourself in the Lord over and over.
- With renewed faith in our God, take the next step you know you should take—even though you're afraid.

The enemy wanted to stop God's plans for the people in Jerusalem, and they used fear to do it. The Israelites strengthened themselves in the Lord and fought back their fear. The wall was completed in a stunning fifty-two days. Now it was time for Israel's enemies to be afraid.

> And when all our enemies heard of it, all the nations around us were afraid and fell greatly in their own esteem, for they perceived that this work had been accomplished with the help of our God. (Nehemiah 6:16)

With God's help, you can fight against fear and win. The Almighty God—who loves us and has plans for us—wants to do great things in our lives. Things that will make the devil and his demons afraid . . . not us.

■ ■ ■

Mark: I had a ton of fear the night before a huge meeting. I got a text from a friend that night that said, "Do it scared." I love the message behind that. We might still feel the fear, but that should never stop us from following through on what we know is right.

What Do I Do When I Feel I'm All Alone?

Sometimes I (Tim) stare at the dark ceiling in my bedroom, thinking I'm the only one awake. It's happened to you too, right? Or maybe your best friends have scattered after graduation, and you feel alone. Maybe a friend turned on you. Or you long for a girlfriend, but that just isn't happening right now. Sometimes it's problems we're facing that make us feel alone—without anyone we can talk to about it. There is no end to situations that can leave us feeling alone.

Truly believing we're alone can lead us down the dark tunnels of despair and fear. Great men of God have felt that, like the prophet Elijah in 1 Kings 19. He thought he was the only man who still followed God in the entire country. Of course, he wasn't.

In 2 Kings 6, the prophet Elisha is in the town of Dothan, surrounded by an enemy army sent to kill him. Elisha's servant felt very alone at that moment and was terrified. But Elisha knew they weren't alone. He said,

> "Do not be afraid, for those who are with us are more than those who are with them." Then Elisha prayed and said, "O Lord, please open his eyes that he may see." So the Lord opened the eyes of the young man, and he saw, and behold, the mountain was full of horses and chariots of fire all around Elisha." (vv. 16–17)

If we're going to rise above the debilitating feeling that we're all on our own, we only need to remember one thing. We're not alone.

"I will never leave you nor forsake you." That's God's promise to us in Hebrews 13:5.

And Psalm 139:7–10 also reminds us that we're never truly alone. "Where shall I go from your Spirit? Or where shall I flee from your presence? If I ascend to heaven, you are there! If I make my bed in Sheol, you are there! If I take the wings of the morning and dwell in the uttermost parts of the sea, even there your hand shall lead me, and your right hand shall hold me."

I love going for bike rides with my kids. As they've gotten older, I give them more freedom to race ahead. But still, without fail, there's a moment when they will take a quick look back, just to make sure I'm still there. Once they see me, they get back to pedaling. It's the same with us. Those verses from Psalm 139 remind us that no matter where we are, we can always look over our shoulder and see God there. It gives us the security to keep our eyes forward and feet pedaling. **—Mark**

As men, when we feel alone, we need to come back to the truth. We're never alone, and Jesus knows exactly what we're going through right now. When we feel we're on our own, let's ask God to open our eyes so that we're assured we aren't alone, and grab hold of that truth in faith.

18

What Do I Do When I'm Stuck in a Bad Situation?

At some point, you will experience it. *Hopelessness.* That feeling of being stuck, with no hope on the horizon. It's overwhelming. I've (Mark) been there. Maybe you're there right now.

It's something the Israelite nation faced. They'd sinned against God, were defeated in battle, and taken captive by other nations. Eventually they were exiled from their land, with no hope of returning. They felt despair . . . overwhelmed with their inability to change their situation.

While in that dark place, God gave the prophet Isaiah a message meant to strengthen a people who had none. See if it does the same for you, today.

> Have you not known? Have you not heard?
> The LORD is the everlasting God, the Creator of the ends of the earth.
> He does not faint or grow weary; his understanding is unsearchable.
> He gives power to the faint, and to him who has no might he increases strength.

Even youths shall faint and be weary, and young men fall exhausted; but they who wait for the LORD shall renew their strength; they shall mount up with wings like eagles; they shall run and not be weary; they shall walk and not faint. (Isaiah 40:28–31)

He describes someone with the power to fly, running without tiring and moving forward without collapsing. Sounds pretty great —and also opposite of anyone's experience when they're feeling hopeless. We're spinning our tires. Exhausted. So how do we get to where Isaiah says we can be? Isaiah gave us three reminders.

Remember who God is: God is everlasting, our Creator, and unsearchable. As we remind ourselves of who God is, we're convinced that God is capable of so much more than we are. With Him as our helper, we have hope of change we could never make happen ourselves.

Remember what God does: God gives power. He renews strength. It's helpful to think back to the times He's shown up for you, or accounts in the Bible of God rescuing people. As we spend time reminding ourselves what God does, we see that our situation is not unfixable. God has done it before. He can do it again!

Remember our role: Isaiah tells them to "wait for the Lord." In other words, quit trying to do this all yourself, or looking for someone else to save you. This job can only be done by God.

In the margins of my Bible, I have a group of dates written next to Isaiah 40. Those were days I sat in that passage completely overwhelmed, weary, and hopeless. Today, each of them represents a personal testimony to the truth of the passage. God does everything Isaiah said He does. I'm here today because I waited for God to take me here. I am only running today because He gave me the strength to move. My hopelessness was no match for God's help.

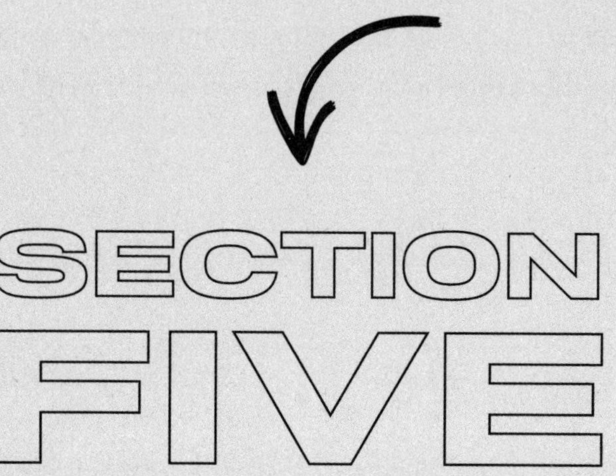

SECTION FIVE

MANHOOD

I've (Tim) learned a ton through good and bad life experiences—and not always my own. Often, I've gained insights on manhood by observing *others*. By taking note of their choices, their actions, and how those work out for them.

Like the time a guy had a bad case of road rage and took it out on my dad. My parents had left my house and were driving in a residential area on their way home. Apparently, my dad didn't take off fast enough after pausing at a stop sign. The driver behind him got impatient—and let my dad know how annoyed he was. Mr. Road Rage whipped around my dad's SUV and cut back into my dad's lane, barely missing the bumper. It scared my dad and mom half to death.

Maybe the driver glanced in the rearview mirror at that moment—to see my dad's face. That's just a guess, but taking his eyes off the road for that split second would explain how he lost control. Mr. Road Rage wasn't able to course-correct quickly enough. His car jumped the curb, plowed down a newly planted maple tree, obliterated a mailbox and its post that was sunk in concrete, then disappeared through an eight-foot privacy hedge.

Badly shaken, my dad drove the last few minutes to his home while Mom phoned me. I raced to meet them—with two of my sons—who were still visiting at the family party.

After making sure my parents were okay and safe at home, my boys and I went back to the spot where everything happened. Police were already on the scene. It turns out that witnesses saw what Mr. Road Rage had done and called 911.

Immediately we spotted the small tree and mailbox the driver had mowed down. We followed the tire ruts through the hedge and found ourselves in someone's front yard. A huge boulder, the size of one of those bean bag chairs, had been hidden by the thick brush. The impact from the car broke the rock in two and sent both halves flying. The massive chunks sat half-buried in the ground like a couple of meteorites. The entire area was littered with broken branches, leaves, and mail. I paced off the distance. Some letters had flown as far as fifty feet from the where the mailbox once stood.

But that wasn't all we found in the debris field. Hitting that boulder did a number on Mr. Road Rage's car. Shattered bits of the vehicle lay scattered on the ground from the mailbox all the way up to a towering shagbark hickory tree. Based on the tracks, the car hit the tree head-on—and shed even *more* body parts. With an impact that hard, likely the driver's airbag deployed. It was impossible to know for sure, because the car was gone. But the ruts from his wheels told us exactly what happened next.

The stunned driver backed up, steered around the tree, and drove across the rest of the lawn onto the driveway. That's where we noticed that the tire tracks changed dramatically. Deep grooves carved into the blacktop driveway showed he was no longer riding on all four tires. He'd blown out at least two of them: as in totally flat. He was now driving on the steel rims. The tracks showed he'd pulled back out onto the road and headed west. It was a sure bet that he wasn't moving nearly as fast as he'd been when he passed my dad, though.

Now who was the slowpoke, right?

Yeah, Mr. Road Rage was gone . . . but the police picked up enough pieces of his car to positively identify the make, model, and color. Sweet justice, right?

Just before my sons and I left the scene where Mr. Road Rage cut my dad off, we discovered the car's license plate in the battered hedge. Apparently, the thing had been ripped off the bumper when Mr. Road Rage hit the big rock. We handed it to the police officer.

The cop smiled. "You just made my day a lot easier." He explained that since the guy had done so much damage to the homeowner's property and then left the scene, he'd be charged with a hit and run. That's serious stuff.

I couldn't help asking. "You think you'll find him?"

"Oh, yeah." The officer waggled the license plate. "We'll get him."

We make plenty of mistakes and learn from them. But let's remember that we can learn from the experiences and choices of others, whether good or bad.

What a great reminder that was to me—and my sons—about the high price of driving like a hothead. Which brings me to this important truth. We don't have to make our own mistakes to learn great life lessons. We can learn from the mistakes of others. We don't have to get drunk to know that's a stupid thing to do. We don't have to hide sin in our life to know that it always comes out and makes a mess. Learning from the experiences of others—good and bad—is one way we can live wise. We see the results of bad decisions and choose a different route ourselves. We see good decisions and choose a similar path. Monkey see, monkey do.

If we want to accelerate our progress toward becoming the men God designed us to be, sometimes all that's needed is to open our eyes and apply what we observe to our life. We learn valuable lessons from the choices others make.

How Does God's Purpose for Manhood Differ from What Culture Is Telling Me?

Some people want you to believe you need to do all kinds of "manly" things to be a man. Wrestle an alligator. Climb Everest. Do hard feats of strength or endurance. Spend hours building our physique at the gym. Give off a rugged vibe.

Others seem to think a *real* man needs to be passively tolerant and accepting of everyone and everything as if that was a more enlightened level of manhood. I (Tim) don't agree with either extreme. They don't describe the core of manhood. They just describe lifestyles.

True manhood is deeper. It has to do with our character. Convictions. Our integrity. It's about our unwavering dedication to God and to following His Word. It's about making personal sacrifices so that we can better help others. We can work out and really *look* good . . . and that does have some value. But when we train and exercise the inside man to be the kind of person God intends us to be? Well, *that* has eternal benefits.

> Train yourself for godliness; for while bodily training is of some value, godliness is of value in every way, as it holds promise for the present life and also for the life to come.
> (1 Timothy 4:7b–8)

True manhood goes way beyond a mature physique. It's about maturing as a Christian inside. It's about training ourselves to become the kind of man of character God designed us to be in all areas of life.

How we use our time and our power.

How we love.

How we handle responsibility.

How we keep our word—and follow His.

How we treat others.

How we use our money—and time.

How we exercise self-discipline to do the right things—even when we think nobody is watching.

Our character says much more about the kind of man we are than so many of the more external things the world often looks to.

I don't typically rank funeral compliments, but if I did, I would put this one at the top: "He was a good man." That one gets me every time. In my mind, that is one of the best things my wife, or one of my kids could ever say about me when I'm gone. Notice, it doesn't focus on externals or accolades. It's entirely about *who they were*, their character. Seeing what we emphasize about a man after they're gone helps me see what matters most about how I live today. **—Mark**

We can learn a lot about manhood when we dig into Bible stories. I think that's one reason why there are so many—especially in the Old Testament. One of my favorites is the story of Boaz in the book of Ruth. The guy was a successful farmer and employer. The backstory opens with the account of Ruth, a young widow. With her husband dead, she no longer had anyone to bring home wages for food and rent. She had to do what she could for food, so she followed Boaz's crew, picking up the scraps of harvested grain they left behind. It was perfectly acceptable to do that back in the day. It would be like dumpster diving behind a restaurant today.

Grab your Bible and check out the book of Ruth. As Boaz enters the story, focus on the kind of character you see in this man. What can you learn about being the man God designed you to be from the story of Boaz? Jot those things down.

We learn from our own choices, for sure. Let's also learn from the examples we see in the Bible—and in life. Let's steer clear of the bad choices people made and put into practice the good. As we do, we'll continue to become the kind of man God designed us to be. And we'll build a good reputation with others—just like Boaz did.

Being a man of character like Boaz was probably didn't come naturally. He had to work at it. I want to be a Boaz. So, I work at it. I build self-discipline. I learn from my experiences—and those of others. The good examples I follow. The bad, I avoid.

If we really want to stand out . . . to be different from so many other men in our world—be a man of character and integrity. It ain't easy, but it's *good*. There'll be times you'll want to react in ways that are totally understandable, natural, or human. But it's not a thing a man of character would do. Listen to the Holy Spirit. Take the high road—even when that means a really tough climb. That is totally man stuff.

Maybe you're a first-generation follower of Christ. Or maybe your dad wasn't much of a man of integrity. You don't have to be the same way. With God's help, you can break that pattern. Learn from what you see in others—good and bad.

My grandpa was a man of integrity. My dad . . . oh my goodness . . . he demonstrated such good character traits. It's my desire too, but it's not something I just inherit. I saw these men work on their Christian character. I saw them as men of character . . . mature Christian men. And boy, did they stand out from so many other men I observed!

There's nothing wrong with going to the gym—although it's not for everyone. But there's one gym all of us need to hit.

That's the one where we build and strengthen the Christian us, the inside us, our *character.* You want to be a man of character, one who matures as a Christian? Good. Me too. I'll see you at the character gym!

Is Masculinity Toxic?

Think of masculinity as the essence of manhood. The DNA. Often, I (Tim) think of masculinity as the God-given *power* or *nature* He's given us as men to provide for those we love, and to protect them. There's nothing toxic about it. Not one thing. It's only when we use our power or when our nature is expressed in ways that *deviate* from God's design that masculinity becomes toxic.

Hollywood shows us plenty of guys using their strength and power to dominate. To put themselves ahead of others or to gain an advantage over them. We see guys like that in life too. But these aren't good examples of being the kind of man God designed us to be. They're often nothing more than examples of masculinity gone bad. Toxic.

Have you ever tasted curdled milk? Gross stuff. One time I poured a bunch of it into a bowl of cereal. I was a few bites in before I noticed. That took me a while to get over! But did I ever have milk again? Of course. Because milk wasn't the problem; milk is great! *The problem was with the milk that went bad.* It's like that with toxic masculinity. Masculinity isn't bad, it's actually great! But in some cases, it goes bad. That's when it should be avoided. **—Mark**

Show me a man who dominates those weaker than he is, and I'll show you someone who is a lousy representative of true masculinity. Show me a man who is self-absorbed, selfish, or proud and arrogant, and I'll bet he's going to be a great example of masculinity gone bad. Show me a man who uses his strength and power for the benefit of Numero Uno instead of helping or serving others, and you can be sure that man will be a poor specimen of true manhood. Show me a man who bottles up his feelings—somehow thinking a man shouldn't express himself in healthy ways—and I'll put money on him missing at least one of the key elements of manhood. Likely he's making life harder on those around him rather than easier. All of these are toxic deviations from true manhood.

Show me a man who dominates those weaker than he is, and I'll show you someone who is a lousy representative of true masculinity.

> Do nothing from selfish ambition or conceit, but in humility count others more significant than yourselves. Let each of you look not only to his own interests, but also to the interests of others. (Philippians 2:3–4)

Because of our sin nature, we have a tendency to go toxic, or to have toxic masculinity moments. This is something real men fight against. As men, we want to use our strength, power, and all our masculinity to serve God and others. The more we put the Foundational Five into practice, the less risk we have of becoming toxic.

How Can I Take Steps to Grow into the Man I'm Supposed to Be?

Let's go back to the story of Boaz in the book of Ruth. The man was all about character and integrity. What did that look like? Here's a list of things I (Tim) wrote in the margins of my Bible.

> *Boaz* ***is described*** *as a "man of standing."* It's not just about success or wealth. The man had earned respect, and we understand why as we read his story. (Ruth 2:1 NIV)
>
> *Boaz* ***acknowledges*** *the little guy.* He starts his day greeting his workers. He's not preoccupied with his own sense of self-importance. (Ruth 2:4)
>
> *Boaz* ***protects and provides*** *for girls/women.* He makes sure Ruth is safe and that she has what she needs—over and over in the story. (Ruth 2:8–9)
>
> *Boaz* ***takes note*** *of and is impressed by Ruth's character, her heart.* It wasn't all about how she looked. He learned to see people beyond the surfacy stuff. (Ruth 2:11)
>
> *Boaz* ***prayed*** *for God's blessing on Ruth.* Praying for the well-being of others—not just about himself? What a man! (Ruth 2:12)
>
> *Boaz* ***makes efforts*** *to see that Ruth isn't embarrassed, even if she messes up.* He makes certain his workers don't give her a hard time in any way. (Ruth 2:15–16)

> *Boaz* ***earned*** *a reputation of being kind to others . . . beyond just his friends.* At this point Ruth was an outsider, yet he didn't make her feel that way. (Ruth 2:13, 20)
>
> *Boaz* ***doesn't do something wrong*** *just to get what he wants.* Taking a wrong shortcut, even for good results, isn't integrity. (Ruth 3:11–13)
>
> *Boaz* ***doesn't waste time*** *when he knows the right thing to do.* He kicks it into gear and gets busy. No stalling. No procrastination. (Ruth 3:18)
>
> *Boaz* ***makes himself accountable*** *to the leaders.* He presents his case and tells them his plans. He wasn't afraid to be honest and open, knowing they'd hold him to his word if he failed to follow through. (Ruth 4:1–12)
>
> *Boaz* ***does what he said he'd do.*** Boaz redeems and rescues Ruth by marrying her. As it turned out, he benefits massively in the process. (Ruth 4:1–13)

All of those good examples of manhood . . . in one story! But it's more than a good story. It's a road map for manhood, guys. It shows what a Christian man looks like: how he talks, how he treats people, and how he grows to be respected.

So, take a fresh look at the manhood principles we find in Boaz. When we compare that to our life, what areas need work? Let's make a list and start there, with His help.

Take a moment to reflect: If your life story was written out like we have for Boaz, what are the things people would say about the kind of man you are? If there are things you wish were true about you, but aren't, take some time to ask God to help you grow in those areas. A lot of the things we see in Boaz we'll talk about in other sections of the book, so keep reading! **—Mark**

What's the Big Mistake Men Make When It Comes to Building Character and Integrity?

I (Tim) drove to Southern Florida to do research for a new fiction series I'd started. I love writing mystery, adventure, suspense . . . thriller stuff. And the Everglades were home to alligators and venomous snakes, which in my opinion are two of the scariest creatures on earth. What a place to set a story, right?

I wanted to see alligators in the wild. Up close. I wanted to see them at night. I wanted to see how their eyes glowed. I wanted to experience some of that fear of being out in the Everglades so that my writing would be more real. I got all that—and so much more than I bargained for. On three occasions I came really, really close to cashing in my chips. One encounter with a twelve-foot male alligator was so terrifying that I couldn't sleep that night. I kept seeing the massive black head of the beast that nearly got me.

Everglades National Park turned out to be one of the creepiest places I'd ever been. The word "park" makes us think of kid-friendly playgrounds, giving a false sense of security. Or the word makes us think of some pristine place, largely untouched by humans. A place of natural beauty so rich that the government protects it. A place where people can enjoy nature. A paradise that developers can't bulldoze and pave.

But after spending time in the Glades, it seemed to me that maybe some parks aren't really about protecting the wildlife from people. Rather, those vast square miles of national park are more about protecting people from the beasts that call those areas home.

The water in the Everglades often looked peaceful and still. Harmless. The trouble was what I saw on the surface didn't reflect at all what lurked beneath it.

Some men spend too much time looking at the surface. When people are watching, they do and say the right things. But who we are as men is not a surface thing.

The big mistake men often make when it comes to building character and integrity? They spend too much time looking at the surface. They're mainly concerned with how they look to others rather than who they really are deep inside. They *appear* to be a man of integrity and character. When people are watching, they do and say the right things. But who we are as men is not a surface thing. So many men fail to go deeper and examine their own heart. They look in the mirror to see how they look to others. Instead, they need to be spending more time looking in the mirror of the Word to see what is really lurking in their own heart.

That's the way it is with some men. On the surface they seem like a decent, aw-shucks kind of guy. But underneath? They're monsters. Rage. Jealousy. Dishonesty. Slander. Pride. Selfishness. For many men, they spend a lot of time and effort hiding who they really are instead of working with God toward changing who they are inside.

We get it. Our society is obsessed with the outward appearance. People often put a lot of effort into how they look on the outside. The clothes they wear, the car they drive, the music they listen to, how fit they are, where they go to school or travel . . . all of it can feed into a strategy of creating an image. It's about projecting a persona of who we want people to *think* we are, not necessarily who we really are inside.

Guys, I'm not saying a man shouldn't be concerned about his outward appearance. But we never want to put more effort into our image than we do working on our true character. Who we are on the *inside.* "Whoever walks in integrity walks securely, but he who makes his ways crooked will be found out" (Proverbs 10:9).

One way to work on the inside is by being in a solid community of believers. The kind of community that knows your weaknesses and flaws and calls you out on it. When we give people the access to our inner self like that, we don't allow the worst parts of us to stay in the shadows. **—Mark**

Eventually, whatever is inside us comes out. Good or bad. When we're tired, when we're hungry, when we're irritated, stressed, or feeling wronged in some way . . . the character flaws inside us come out faster and easier.

What about us, my friend? Where do we need to work on our character and integrity?

Are we honest—telling the whole truth every time? Even if it would be easy to fudge the facts a bit? Even when telling the truth will get us into big trouble?

Do we keep our word? Do we do what we said we'll do—without needing to be reminded? Are we dependable that way?

Do we notice those who don't have the same advantages we have—and look for ways to help?

Are we using our power to make life easier for others —or are we mainly thinking about ourselves?

How do we talk to and about others?

Are we kind to others—even those we don't know?

Do we have a habit of doing the right and honorable thing once we realize what that is—and not stalling it off?

It's easy to get sucked into the trap of thinking that becoming better at some sport or working out more will make us more of a man. We end up building our manhood on the wrong foundation. The more important characteristics of manhood are built on character and integrity. That's why Boaz is such a great example of a man, in my opinion. When you read the previous section, did you make a list of things you wanted to work on? Ask God to help you be that kind of man—and keep the list close.

Is Gentleness Just a Nice Way to Admit Weakness?

When it comes to things we'd like to be known for, gentleness doesn't make our cut. We don't put it on our list of traits we hope comes through during a job interview. It doesn't make our list of character qualities we aspire to possess. We can't imagine it being high on a list of what girls are looking for in a guy. I've never seen it make one of those lists highlighting top traits of a good leader.

Gentleness is the underdog of all character qualities. If we could all choose one of the fruits of the Spirit to consistently be a 10 out of 10 in our life, how many of us would choose gentleness?

I (Mark) have a theory. The reason gentleness is so underrated is because it's wildly misunderstood. We don't see gentleness as a positive. It's more likely a compliment we give to someone who wasn't great enough to get to the top. It's a way to find something nice to say about someone who isn't strong enough to have other—more important—things affirmed. Gentleness has become the silver lining quality in a pushover. We see gentleness as weak. It's soft. It's the guy who is mousy and doesn't speak up for himself or others.

Let's recalibrate our idea of gentleness with a quick look at how the Bible talks about it.

- Jesus, the one who took on the powerful leaders, flipped over tables, walked on water, defeated legions of demons, fought off every attack of the devil, and chose to suffer on the cross so that he could save us—called Himself gentle

(Matthew 11:29). If that's part of His character, gentleness must mean something beyond weakness.

- God, who encourages us to be strong, unafraid, and zealous for Him, is looking to produce gentleness in our life. That can't suggest a contradiction. His Spirit works every day to produce more of it in your heart (Galatians 5:22–23).

- Jesus taught that the meek (another word for gentle) will inherit the earth (Matthew 5:5). They're the ones who'll be the survivors in a tough world.

- Paul was a tough man. In Philippians 4:5 (NIV), this man's man who had survived shipwrecks, endured beatings, thrived in tough prisons, and was an assassination target, encourages the church to "Let your gentleness be evident to all."

Okay, so gentleness is not weak. It shouldn't be a compliment we sort of wish we didn't get. But if it's not weakness, what is it?

When our third child was born, he came into the world at 3 pounds, 15 ounces. I'd never seen a baby that small before. The hospital gave him a little knit hat for newborns. The hat fit like a sock over a marble. He was so frail and weak.

Then came the day we brought Gabe home to meet our other kids. I'll never forget that moment when our six-year-old rough-and-tough boy held tiny Gabe. As James cradled Gabe, he embodied gentleness. James had more strength and power than Gabe, but he harnessed his power and put it under control as he held the vulnerable. That is gentleness. It's power . . . under control.

When we have strength, authority, and the ability or opportunity to flex our strength? Gentleness is when we choose to channel the strength in a controlled manner. Gentleness is when all of our power is put into submission or control—to be used in ways that benefit those around us. Especially the weak and vulnerable.

I never wanted gentleness to describe me until the day of my grandpa's funeral. As we told stories about his life, I finally had a working definition of gentleness. He had power in his job, and yet he used his authority for the good of others. He had strength in his finances and resources, yet he controlled them in a way that blessed others and benefited God's kingdom. He had a way of honoring those around him as he used what he had to lift them up. In his gentleness, he took all his strength and let it bless and benefit the world, instead of wielding it in harmful and destructive ways—or just using it for his own benefit.

Gentleness was Jesus, as He hung on the cross. He had the power to come down and save Himself. But He put His power under control and hung there for our benefit. His gentleness led to an amazing victory over death and saving us from our sin. There's nothing weak about that.

We live in a world of flexing men pushing, controlling, and manipulating their way through life. Imagine a world of men using their position and authority in gentle ways; there's another way. A better way. Let's put our power under control and embrace gentleness. Those who find the strength to do that will inherit the earth.

■ ■ ■

Tim: True gentleness is great strength. We've all seen the crazy driver using the power of his car to get ahead by cutting others off, tailgating, and making fast lane changes. That isn't strength. That's self-serving. That's weakness. The stronger drivers let somebody merge in ahead of them. They may pull onto the shoulder to help jump a car with a dead battery—or to help some bewildered driver change a tire. Let's use our strength, abilities, influence, and opportunities for the good of others—and for God's kingdom. How do we actually become gentle in those strong ways? It starts with talking to God about it. Asking Him to help us become strong, gentle men. And we have His Holy Spirit to nudge us that way. The Spirit wants to strengthen our gentleness. Let's be sure we're paying attention to those prompts from the Spirit!

Am I Really Supposed to Be a Protector—Especially When So Many Women Don't Want to Be Protected?

Yep. Generally speaking, God made men with the genetics to be bigger and stronger than most females. There were reasons for that. One of them certainly is that men are the protectors. And protecting others isn't limited to getting physical, like getting into a fight. It's much bigger than that.

When we hear of terrorists or extremists who kill women and children, our blood boils as men. When we hear of men who enslave women and children in the human trafficking industry, we see that as being completely vile and evil. God didn't create men to be bigger and stronger so that they'd have an easier time dominating or exploiting women and children. Deep down, I'm (Tim) absolutely convinced God designed us men to be protectors.

When asked which commandment was the most important commandment, Jesus gave the top two.

> And he said to him, "You shall love the Lord your God with all your heart and with all your soul and with all your mind. This is the great and first commandment. And a second is like it: You shall love your neighbor as yourself." (Matthew 22:37–39)

The word "neighbor" was clearly defined by Jesus in a parable as being anyone in need . . . whether friend or enemy. A neighbor can be someone we know or a complete stranger.

We're to love others. The word "love" packs a lot of meaning, but check out what Scripture says about it here. "Love bears all things, believes all things, hopes all things, endures all things" (1 Corinthians 13:7).

Love bears all things. That doesn't mean that we just take an attack and endure it without complaint. But think instead of a support beam in a mine that bears the weight of rocks and earth above it. That beam keeps the tunnel from collapsing and ensures the miners are safe. Or think of a submarine, bearing the pressure of the water around it. It keeps everyone inside safe and dry. Think of Jesus, bearing the weight of our sins on the cross—so that we could be saved . . . protected from eternal punishment in hell. So, spiritually, emotionally, or physically . . . in other words, come hell or highwater, a man bears whatever is needed to protect others.

That four-word sentence, *love bears all things,* helps make our job as men easier. It helps us cut through moments of indecision in so many situations. We know what we're to do. To be the support. The protection. To do for others what they can't do for themselves.

Let's imagine we've got a brother, sister, or friend getting involved in something that's truly bad for them—or dangerous. Maybe it's something wrong, and they expect you to keep their secret. That's how they want you to protect them. But is anything they do a secret from God? Might their bad choices put them in a position to miss God's blessing in their life—or warrant God's discipline? If we really want to protect them, we must urge them to repent . . . to change direction. And if they don't, might the best way to protect them be talking to someone who *can* help them? Protecting others isn't always easy—or appreciated. But it's what God designed us to do.

This reminds me a bit of Adam. He was *with* Eve in the garden when she ate the fruit. Adam knew it was wrong and didn't stop her. He didn't protect Eve in this situation, and they both reaped heavy consequences (along with the rest of us). **—Mark**

Or picture this. We're on some social media platform, and friends are trashing a person who isn't even in the conversation. Maybe we resist the urge to pile on. Good. But is that enough? Is that all we have to do to protect—simply not join in? Could we say something nice about the person? Or ease the group onto another topic? Wouldn't either of those options do more to protect that person?

Or what about this scenario? You're with a girl, and you're feeling the temptation to go on a little exploring expedition. And the girl actually seems willing. But is that protecting her? God made her, and the best thing for her is to save herself in every way for the man who marries her. God has made us protectors . . . so, how will I protect that girl—even in this situation—even if she doesn't seem to want it?

Men in our world have massively lost touch with God's design for them.

Have you ever noticed how many movies show men who are protectors—and others who play it safe instead? Who are we cheering for? Who do we wish we could imitate? Deep down we admire the protectors . . . because God created *us* with the heart to protect others.

Men in our world have massively lost touch with God's design for them. When a calamity happens, a man's instinct should be to jump in to help or protect. To be a beam, protecting others from a crushing situation. But today, many men are more likely to grab their phone and *video* whatever is happening than they are to help. I saw a clip on a social media platform recently where some guy seemed almost giddy with his own sense of self-importance at capturing a crisis situation on his camera. I'm watching it, in partial disbelief. *Why is he filming? Why isn't he helping that person? Why would he post this video that shows his first reaction was to get a video rather than to help in a moment of crisis?*

We talked earlier about Boaz, a great example of godly

manhood. He made sure Ruth was protected in a number of ways. Guys . . . let's be protectors. God can help you, because He's designed you to be one!

What if I Try to Protect Someone and It's Not Welcomed?

This happens more and more in our mixed-up world. I've (Tim) sometimes found that simple gestures of courtesy are not always taken as intended. If that happens to you, don't overreact or make assumptions. Some women do have issues with these things, but it is not your problem.

Let's not let another person's issues with men keep us from doing what we were designed to do. If we step up in some way to make life easier for a woman, and they reward us with a scathing comment? Let's take it like a man. We've got broad shoulders, right?

■ ■ ■

Mark: It's often the motive behind our protection that gets so misunderstood in our culture. If I step up and protect a woman, my motive is often perceived as demeaning, when in reality it's driven by love (1 Corinthians 13:5–7). Some of the systems of our world have valued women less over the years, so we get some of their pushback. But we shouldn't hold back our responsibility to love and protect because many people have made women out to be less throughout history. As we protect, our love isn't demeaning; it's a beacon of light highlighting their equal value as an image bearer.

■ ■ ■

I (Tim) love the Old Testament story in the book of Joshua where two Israelite spies were pinned down on Rahab's rooftop, a resident of the city of Jericho. Rehab believed God was going to give the city to the Israelites—and hid the spies from the soldiers scouring Jericho for them. The grateful spies promised to protect her and her family when the Israelites raided the walled city. But they made it clear that they'd only protect the lives of Rahab's family members who stayed inside her home once the battle began. Those who rejected the spies' offer of protection would be on their own. The spies would bear no guilt for what would happen to Rahab or anyone in her family who stepped outside the boundaries of their protection.

Rahab was wise and accepted their protection. Rahab and her entire family were saved. But not everyone we meet will be that way. If we try to protect someone, and they pull back from us? We're released from that duty to protect. We must be about whatever it is that God has us to do. We are protectors, but largely can only protect those who are open to it.

Who needs protecting in your life? How will you take steps toward doing exactly that?

When Should I Speak My Mind—and When Should I Keep My Opinions to Myself?

Much of the time, the best thing we can do with our opinions is keep them to ourselves. That can be *really* hard to do. But there are reasons the Bible says "Let every person be quick to hear, slow to speak, slow to anger" (James 1:19). Being quick at giving our opinion isn't always wise. Here are some examples of when I (Tim) feel expressing our opinion may be a mistake.

When our motive isn't stellar. Do we want to impress someone, or put someone down?

When we're venting, in a rush, or can't say it in love. Opinions given when we're angry or hurried generally lead to saying things we regret—or should.

Before we've heard all the facts. Especially if someone is asking for our opinion. We have to be so careful to be sure we've got the whole story.

When we're around someone who is playing the fool. Proverbs 18:2 reminds us of the futility of reasoning with a fool. "A fool takes no pleasure in understanding, but only in expressing his opinion." Here are some examples to help us recognize fools:

They don't seem interested in learning what God has to say about things.

They tend to make bad choices and hurt others without remorse.

They're set in their opinions and argue with (or bully) anyone who disagrees.

They blame others for their situation, rarely admitting that their own choices and mistakes put them where they are.

So when *should* we give our opinion?

When our opinion will encourage someone else.

When our opinion will nudge someone in the right direction . . . or keep them from sinning or making a terrible mistake. The Bible talks about being an "iron sharpens iron" friend. Sharpening an iron tool often creates sparks. And that can happen between friends when you express an opinion they don't want to hear.

When someone asks our opinion—not to debate us—but because they're legitimately looking for input or advice.

When we feel God leading us to say something in a loving way.

Why Is It So Important to Be Careful with Our Words?

If someone has a concealed carry license, you expect them to be really careful with how they handle that firearm, right? A gun is a powerful weapon that can protect or can destroy others. Words are no different.

If we're following God's plan for manhood, it's important that we're careful with that weapon holstered in our jaw. The Bible is clear about how important this issue is to God. When I (Tim) was a kid, there was a wise saying I heard often: "If you can't say something nice, don't say anything at all." The Bible says there is "a time to keep silence, and a time to speak" (Ecclesiastes 3:7). As men desiring to follow God, we need to get that right.

The Bible tells us we're to do everything in love, and that includes how we talk to others. Are the words that come out of our mouth (or the words we text) short, rude, critical, or downright mean sometimes? That's a problem. Whatever comes out of our mouth is an indicator of what's in our heart. Whatever we say—or want to say—gives us a pretty good idea of where we are spiritually—and where we need work.

The good news? God can help us know when to speak, when to stay quiet—if we ask Him. He can help us know what to say, how to say it, and when.

■ ■ ■

One way I (Mark) have gotten help from God in this area, is to pray Psalm 19:14. It says, "Let the words of my mouth and the meditation of my heart be acceptable in your sight." Yes, David, the writer of this psalm, wants God to be pleased with his words. But he goes deeper and asks for God to help him address the thoughts that will one day become his words. Would God be pleased with the way you speak, *and* the running dialogue in your head?

28

Short of Using Duct Tape and Super Glue, How Can I Do a Better Job of Keeping My Mouth Shut When I Should?

Let me (Mark) start with a couple of Bible verses to guide our thinking; then we'll get into some practical ways to apply it.

"Let every person be quick to hear, slow to speak, slow to anger; for the anger of man does not produce the righteousness of God" (James 1:19–20).

"Whoever guards his mouth preserves his life; he who opens wide his lips comes to ruin" (Proverbs 13:3).

The Bible has a lot to say about *what* we say. No matter our personality, the example we saw growing up, what our workplace, school, or dorm environment is . . . we're all called to the same standard. The Bible calls us to control our words and use them in ways that build people up.

How are we actually doing with this? Quick show of hands, how many of us would describe ourselves as "quick to speak and slow to hear"? How many of us don't put a guard on our mouth, but are more of the "loose lips sink ships" type?

■ ■ ■

"I could have gone all day without saying that." I (Tim) remember a man saying that seconds after he'd made a nasty comment. He regretted what he said the moment the words came out of his mouth. Often, it's when we speak too quickly that we get ourselves in trouble. We share our opinion or criticism without taking time to think through if this is the best time, place, or way to do it. We say something that hurts someone because we didn't take time to consider how our comment might impact them.

I love Proverbs 12:18. "There is one whose rash words are like sword thrusts, but the tongue of the wise brings healing." I used to love getting a little jab in—and getting laughs from others. But I'm sure I hurt people a whole lot more than I realized. Now I work hard—exercising a little self-control and Holy Spirit–control—at being the man described in the second half of that verse. I want to be wise with what I say. I want to encourage others. I want to help them be the person God designed them to be. That goes for the things I write or post too. Sometimes just not being so quick to speak is all that's needed for the Holy Spirit to help us avoid sarcasm, rudeness, and belittling, angry, and generally hurtful words—and the regrets they bring.

■ ■ ■

Our goal is to slow the flow of our words to make sure what comes out is beneficial for others. Here are my (Mark) top five ways you can start practicing that today:

> **Grow in Holy Spirit–control.** This goes back to our Foundational Five. If the fruit of the Spirit is growing in our heart, then we'll be speaking in more and more loving and patient ways. Does being slow to speak seem impossible? That's one reason God put His Spirit inside of you. Ask Him to help.
>
> **Have a go-to line**. Come up with a line to be a buffer between how you feel and what you say. Something

like "I need to think about that," or "I think we should talk about something else," or "I'm not ready to talk about that." When we do this, we create some space to get our words in order.

Ask questions. One easy way to slow down our words, is to ask more questions. This will help us get an accurate view of everything before we comment on it. You might be surprised how much more level-headed our response is when we have more details.

Know what to avoid. We tend to be more sensitive or passionate about certain topics (politics, other family members, past hurts or mistakes). When those come up, self-control and discretion are hard to come by. It's wise to acknowledge our weakness and approach any conversation on those topics with caution. I'm not saying to avoid tough conversations that we don't enjoy, but rather to take inventory of the topics we struggle to talk through in a godly way. We should put these conversations off to the side until we can handle them in a mature way.

Know who to avoid. I'm not giving you a pass here to avoid talking to the people you don't like. I'm thinking more about the argumentative types who seem incapable of having decent conversations. We've tried over and over, and they continue to drive discussions to heated arguments. Part of keeping our words in check could very well involve avoiding dialogue with the people who bait us or tend to bring out our worst.

What Are the Things That Can Destroy a Man?

As a kid, I (Tim) loved Superman. The fictional superhero possessed the strength do a world of good. But Kryptonite was the one thing that could weaken or destroy him. So, he was careful to stay far away from Kryptonite.

As Christian men, God empowers us with all that we need to do the superhuman things He's planned for us. But there are things that can weaken or destroy us—and consequently derail us from becoming the man He intended us to be.

So how do we avoid our Kryptonite? Jesus warns us in Matthew 5:29–30 not to toy with anything that can hurt us spiritually. We're to be brutal. Aggressive. Relentless. We're to cut those things right out of our life. We're to declare war, in a very real sense.

How do we do that?

First, know what has the ability to pull you from God. What keeps you from His Word—or from obeying it? What weakens your ability to be the man of character and integrity that He's designed you to be? Screen time? Games? Porn? Certain friendships? Make a list.

Second, work on strategies to combat those things—or replace them with better choices. To help arm you for combat, go back to the start of this book and review the Foundational Five. Especially look at the sections on self-control and Holy Spirit–control.

Sometimes we flirt with our Kryptonite, seeing how close we can actually come without suffering the negative effects. Not smart. That's a great way to undo everything God wants for us as men. Let's steer clear of our Kryptonite, and we'll be amazed at the superhuman ways He'll strengthen us to be the man He's designed us to be.

30

Why Should I Care What Others Think of Me?

If we're followers of Christ, we're ambassadors of Christ. It shouldn't take long before anyone who knows me (Tim), you—or knows *of* us—becomes keenly aware that we're followers of His. And once they know this, anything we say or do is a reflection on the One we claim to be dedicated to. Philippians 2:14–16 reminds us that we're to be His light in this dark, depraved world. What others see in us ought to make them want to learn more about Christ. Sometimes the only impression some will get of God is what they see in us.

A good reputation with other followers of Christ gives them an example to follow.

First Timothy 4:12 mentions five areas for us to be a good example to other believers. "Let no one despise you for your youth, but set the believers an example in speech, in conduct, in love, in faith, in purity." The way we talk, behave, how we love others, our level of faith in God, our dedication to be pure. In all these areas we should excel and be an inspiration for others to follow.

A good reputation is also incredibly valuable. Protect it. Our reputation helps people trust us. I can think of many men over the years who've been offered or denied great opportunities—based on their reputation.

How can we build and protect our reputation?

Don't do stupid things. Focus on doing the right and better things—all the time. What happens in Vegas doesn't stay in Vegas. Eventually, it gets out.

Be dependable. Do what we say we'll do—without needing reminders.

Be trustworthy—like when someone confides in us.

Be honest. Hold tight to integrity.

Do the right things—even when nobody is watching.

Show kindness to others—even those who aren't our friends.

Be a gentleman and protector on a date.

Show honor to our parents.

Show respect to those in authority over us.

Do what we're asked to do without complaining or arguing.

See what needs to be done—and do it without being asked.

Put into practice the things we read in the Bible.

Work hard—and do good work.

All these and more are part of building a good reputation. Build it right, and a good reputation will absolutely open all kinds of doors for us that'd be locked tight otherwise.

You're thinking about so many things right now. Building for a future. Getting an education. Starting your career. Finding that Christian girl who'll love you and stand by your side for life. But here's a secret *so* many young men miss. Too many are fixed on having fun, building influence, pursuing interests, expanding their education, or making money. Many seem to think that pursuing these will solve all their problems and make life better. It doesn't work that way. Build a good reputation, and you'll *avoid* a lot of problems—and life will likely be much better.

"A good name is to be chosen rather than great riches, and favor is better than silver or gold" (Proverbs 22:1).

Remember Boaz, the man we mentioned when talking about character and integrity? That man had a *really* good reputation—which helped him in many ways. Others respected him. Trusted him. And one of the greatest benefits? He got a terrific wife as a direct result of the kind of man he was.

Oh yeah . . . your reputation is important and valuable. Build it carefully. Protect it from your own tendency to ruin it. Your efforts will pay off, and your good reputation will help you in countless ways.

How far should we go to defend our reputation? Often, not nearly as far as we might think. Sure, there are times I've talked with somebody to straighten out a rumor. That may be fine. But so often people just say nasty things—or are quick to misjudge us. If we defend our good name every time that happens, we'll often appear defensive, which tarnishes our reputation even more.

Jesus' reputation took a beating when he started hanging out with guys like Zacchaeus, and other "sinners." People couldn't believe he made deliberate efforts to be with . . . *them*. Did Jesus try to save face, play both sides, or keep up a good image with the religious folk? Nah. He pointed them to what was right without getting caught up trying to save His reputation. **—Mark**

Defending our reputation can be a distraction. An exit ramp on the highway of life. A few years ago, someone trashed me in an online forum because they totally misunderstood something I wrote. That was devastating to me, especially because they got it wrong. But the fact that they chose to put that out on a public forum rather than contacting me directly—like through my website—showed they weren't following God's clear directions in His Word. How likely would they be open to what I'd say if they were already ignoring what God said? And to defend my reputation by responding to them on the online forum could easily be seen as me being defensive, especially since it would be hard to convey my tone there.

Sometimes we have to let it go, trusting God to protect us and our reputation. King David does this over and over in the book of Psalms. We're God's kids, and we're often way better off asking Him to take care of it.

Let's focus our energies on building a good reputation instead of defending ourselves. And honestly, there'll be times others trash you, even when you do the right things. Resist the urge to pay them back or retaliate in some way (1 Peter 3:8–17). Keep doing the right things, and often those who slander us will be ashamed.

I Have a Tendency to Compare Myself to Other Men. How Do I Keep That Under Control?

I (Mark) still remember the day I realized I wasn't making it into the NBA. I was attending a basketball summer camp a few weeks before I started freshman year in high school. The camp gave me a chance to impress the coach before tryouts and some time to scope out the talent.

They were good. Like, way-better-than-me good. I remember assigning the team roster spots in my head based on my observations. I hoped there would be a spot for me, but I wasn't sure; there were so many others that I believed were better than I was.

During a water break I asked one of them if he planned on going to the NBA. I'll never forget Pat's response. "None of us are going to the NBA." If the best point guard in the gym saw it as *that* obvious, then it must be true! I took another sip from my water bottle and nodded, as if what he said was also my shared opinion, not my shattered dream.

You ever been there before? I'm not talking about a shattered NBA dream (although I'm sure some of you can relate). Have you ever found your mind in a deep game of comparison? There's no limit to ways we can compare ourselves to other men. Our job, car, body, income, grades, scholarships, girlfriend, or how well we can stack furniture in a moving van. C'mon this is getting out of control, isn't it?

We compare all the time, and not just about trivial stuff. It's deeper things, too. How well we're liked. Our basic personality.

Our secret insecurities. Maybe the families we were born into or the potential opportunities we see or don't see for our future. We compare ourselves with other men's life success and wonder why we're left sitting on the bench.

There's no limit to ways we can compare ourselves to other men.

Is it helpful to know you aren't the only one doing this? We all stack ourselves up against other guys. And when we do, we leave that mental study session either high with our own success and progress or discouraged with how far behind the rest of the pack we are.

We want to be the one who has more, is doing it better, and is more liked. If we find even one person beating us in any of those categories, the comparison game takes over.

There are no winners in the comparison game. If we feel the other guy is better than us in some area, we open ourselves up to the cancerous dangers of jealousy or discouragement. We might keep digging until we find some area of our life that we have the edge on that other person. That completely derails the focus we should have as men—and opens the door for pride. When we compare ourselves to other men like this, we'll generally come out the loser. **—Tim**

It matters that we get a handle on this. Think about how it affected great men in the Bible.

- Moses questioned God's calling on his life to free the Israelites from Egypt. Why? Because he couldn't speak well, compared to others. He thought another man would be better for the job.

- Saul lost the game of comparison to David and was consumed with jealousy.
- The prodigal son left home and foolishly spent his entire inheritance on partying and sin. Afterward, he returned home broken and ashamed, but was still welcomed by his dad. The prodigal's brother, who'd faithfully served his dad and was in line to inherit all his dad owned, got himself caught in the comparison trap. Maybe the son who'd never left home saw all the fun he'd missed and failed to see how really good he had it. But he got angry and missed the chance to celebrate how his brother had been restored to the family—and in essence had come back from the dead.

Comparing ourselves to others is a game that will lead to great frustration and loss if we let it. Here's a few ways we can fight this comparison battle in our heads.

Build up the foundation. Every one of the Foundational Five is helpful for this—but maybe none more than "Knowing your purpose." The more confident and satisfied you are in the purpose that God has given you, the fewer reasons you have to compare yourself to the life and purposes He's given to others. And the more you're living out that purpose, the fewer reasons you'll have to stack your achievements up against others.

Expose the fickleness of comparison. When you think about it, our game of comparison is a horrible assessment of reality. Reminding ourselves of this will help us fight hard against the habit of comparing ourselves to other men.

- When we compare, we're usually harder on ourselves than those we're comparing ourselves to. We see our faults or shortcomings, but we can't possibly know all the ways others come up short as compared to us.
- Notice how often you make up or assume what the other person would do in a situation. "I bet they never do this . . . or always do that." We're comparing ourselves to a standard that doesn't even exist!
- Comparison happens too often with people we've never met. We look at a polished version of them online and think we should be the same.
- We compare other people's best moments and line it up against our worst.

Replace our competitor with a rabbi. Instead of trying to be better than someone out of a place of envy and comparison, find someone you admire and then learn to live more like them. Think about Paul in 1 Corinthians 11:1 when he says, "Follow my example, as I follow the example of Christ." He wanted people to follow his lead and learn from him, not out of shame and comparison, but out of a place of respect, honor, and admiration. This is the biblical way to imitate others, as a disciple looking to learn from a rabbi.

Pray for them. Sometimes I've hoped to see someone be unsuccessful so that I feel better about myself. I inwardly cheer as they take a misstep or miss an opportunity. The quickest way to fix my heart here is to pray for their well-being and blessing. Jesus told us to pray for our enemies, and I wonder if the person we compare ourselves to is a bigger villain in our mind than we admit.

One more thing . . . limit your time on social media. The posts we see absolutely beg us to compare our everyday life to the excitement of someone else's. Even a post that is absolutely true gives the false impression that this guy's life is overflowing with great things. The reality is that someone's post represents what . . . maybe a terrific two minutes of their day or week? The rest of their time was probably just as unremarkable as ours was. **—Tim**

How Do I Become the Hero I Look Up To?

I (Mark) love trees. If you didn't have an image in your head of what I look like, I'm guessing you're imagining me as a middle-aged bird watching enthusiast . . . binoculars, vest, cargo shorts . . . the whole look. I'm not at that level (yet). I just love trees.

It started back in my early twenties when my family spent the day in Muir Woods National Monument. Standing at the base of Redwoods towering over two hundred feet tall grabbed my attention. I hadn't given much thought to trees before that day, but seeing how massive these things had grown blew me away.

The average age of the Redwoods I saw that day? Six hundred years old. Their maturity had been a process. It took time for those trees to become strong and so they're impressive to look at. And the same can be said of our heroes. We look up to these men of God, strong in their faith and, in a spiritual sense, towering over us. But it took time for them to become that way.

If you want to be like that man of God you look up to, the first step is to embrace the process. You can't separate the character that inspires us to look up to them from the years it took to grow to that stature. Maturity and time are connected. Redwoods have weathered heat, cold, and storms, season after season. All these combined to make them strong. They sunk roots deep below to get the water and minerals they needed and grew a thick canopy overhead to get the needed sunlight. Any man worth imitating has had years of God developing them and adding branches to hold the fruit they possess.

We want that process to be instant, like a one-click "Buy Now" button online. We admire their faith/character/wisdom and the respect they've gained. We see how it would benefit us today, in this season. The idea of having to potentially wait years for this—or anything in our culture—is so foreign we tend to lose motivation to pursue it. If it takes time, we push it off our radar for something more immediately attainable and gratifying. Let the example of our hero be the motivation to set our sights on something greater and awe-inspiring . . . the spiritual strength that happens over a lifetime.

But embracing the process isn't just a "wait it out" approach. As if you could wake up one day and you've become someone great.

Go back to the tree for a second. That tree received sunshine from above, along with water and nutrients from the soil below every single day for its entire life. This is what caused it to grow. We need the same. Jesus explained the secret to spiritual growth in John 15. In that analogy, he compared all of us to branches and compared himself to the vine that supported the branches and brought them the nutrients they needed. His point was simple. If you want to grow, you need to stay connected to Jesus.

I can guarantee you, any Christian man you look up to has made it a habit to stay connected to Jesus. They've built daily routines and habits around spending time with God. They've disciplined themselves to find their nutrients there instead of chasing what the world offers. Their consistency to these habits over time has set their course to be the massive tree of faith we see today.

■ ■ ■

Tim: Years ago, an older man I knew described a time he'd crossed a place known as Rattlesnake Canyon. He'd wanted to get to a bluff on the other side where he'd have some one-on-one time with God. He believed if he did that, he'd have a mountaintop experience that would accelerate his growth. But that mountaintop "feeling" didn't happen. He was disappointed, but over time learned that his real Christian growth and strength came more slowly. It was just as Mark described . . . consistently staying connected to God over the long haul. I saw that in my own dad. His years of staying true to Jesus—and living out the Foundational Five—grew him into a redwood of a Christian.

There's something about being in a redwood forest that's

amazing. The air is fresher. The atmosphere calmer. There's a sense of safety there. A giant redwood doesn't have to say a word for you to know it possesses massive strength. It's obvious. Some men seem to constantly be trying to prove to everyone around them that they're worthy of hero status. But the real heroes don't have to prove anything—and you won't either. Stay connected to Jesus, and He'll grow you into a redwood . . . a hero of a Christian man.

■ ■ ■

I (Mark) see guys struggle with this all the time. They lack consistency in their time with God and then wonder why they so easily fall into temptation. Their time with God is sporadic, and they wonder why they feel far from God. They read their Bible for a week or two, but don't see big results . . . so they lose sight of its value. Let your hero be a visual to you of the benefits of consistent good habits over time in your life.

A good place to start with all of this could be spending time with that man you look up to and asking him what his time with God has looked like over the course of his lifetime. Learn what he did, and how he did it and start applying that into your life. You might be surprised to see what that grows into a decade from now.

SECTION
SIX

THE CHURCH

The first novel I (Tim) ever wrote was set in the medieval English countryside. An editor gave an honest assessment of my writing—and there was something he said that stuck with me.

"Have you ever actually *visited* this area that you're writing about?"

I shook my head. "But I've read books. Looked at pictures. Studied the online videos of others who have."

It was obvious by his face that he wasn't impressed with the hours I'd spent watching and listening. He handed me back my manuscript.

"Your writing lacks a sense of *place*."

Sure, I'd learned a ton about the location where my story was set, but I hadn't actually *been* there. I could answer almost any question someone might have thrown at me about the location, but I'd never experienced it. There was something hollow about that story. I was writing about a place I'd never truly been. That book was never published.

Believe me, I did things different with my writing from then on. Whether a story took place in the Florida Everglades or at the bottom of the ocean, I learned that I needed to go there and experience it for myself before I could write about it.

There is an important parallel with this aspect of writing—and to the whole issue of going to church.

Why Is It Essential for a Man to Go to Church? Can't I Just Listen Online or Do a Bible Study at Home?

Being in church and experiencing everything there in person is vastly different from viewing the service online. It's the difference between standing outside watching through a window and going inside and actually *being* part of it. If I'm not meeting with other believers, what we often call *going to church,* there will be something missing in my life.

The Bible is clear that God wants us to actually *meet* with other believers—not settle for simply viewing church services.

"And let us consider how to stir up one another to love and good works, not neglecting to meet together, as is the habit of some, but encouraging one another, and all the more as you see the Day drawing near" (Hebrews 10:24–25).

Besides the obvious point of this being a command, there are good reasons why it's important that we actually meet with other believers. Here are two.

> **For our protection.** Being with other believers strengthens our faith. We're more likely to stay on track —or get back on the right path more quickly. When we're surrounded by Christians, we see others going through tough times, testing, or temptations—just like us. Often, that helps us face whatever it is we're facing.
>
> **For the protection of others.** Going to church isn't just about what we get out of the service or worship. We're to "stir up one another to love and good works." We're to encourage others to stay on the right paths. To make good choices. Sometimes we encourage others without even knowing it, just because they see we're there.

I can't tell you the number of times I've walked into church with a hard heart, bad attitude, or sin that needed convicting. It's a lot . . . like more than 10. I've experienced that first point, "for our protection," on so many of those mornings. That routine of showing up and being with God's people has proven to be one of the most important things I've done to remain faithful to God over the years. **—Mark**

We've got an enemy who strategizes to tear us apart, right? We dare not forget that. Going to church will help us—and others—be strong. To resist him.

The verses we mentioned from Hebrews warn us not to be "neglectful" when it comes to attending church. To be neglectful is to be careless. Sloppy. Shirking our duties or responsibilities. Inconsistent.

This passage reminds us that the closer we get to His return, the more dedicated we should be to getting to church. Maybe that's because our culture will be growing worse and worse, and we'll need the strength we'll get by gathering with other believers.

Way back in the book of Genesis, God said it wasn't good for man to be alone. In that context, he was talking about Adam needing a mate. I think the same principle can apply when it comes to our spiritual life, guys. Yes, of course we need to study our Bible at home for ourselves. But doing this Christian life alone isn't the way God designed it to work. We also need to be gathering with a community of believers regularly for their good and protection—and ours.

34

What Do I Do if I've Been Hurt by People at the Church?

This is such an important question. I (Mark) gotta admit, I feel some tension answering it. I say that for two reasons.

First? It's personal. I've experienced the hurt and disappointment that sometimes happens within the church. The wounds went deep and took years for me to work through. I know what it takes to walk that road. How can I possibly share in a short response something that would help you walk yours?

Second, cliché answers have a way of seeping into our responses to questions like this. If you've been hurt by the church or its leaders, the quick and predictable answers tend to push you away before ever being helpful. I know what I am about to say in the paragraphs below is not earth-shattering. How can I connect this truth, as simple as it seems, in a way that isn't easily dismissed?

My wife was out with a friend, talking about some of the ways we'd been hurt by other believers. They had the luxury of good coffee and pastries to enjoy over their conversation. I wish I had that for ours today. As they were talking, my wife's friend asked, "How did you not walk away from God, or the church?"

It's our question today, just with different wording. If you've been hurt, disappointed, and betrayed . . . what do you do?

My wife responded, "You have to make the decision . . . you either believe in God, or you don't."

That's it.

I know, I know, I said I didn't want to be cliché. And that sounds too simple to be useful. But I am telling you, it's right. As basic as her response was, it's packed with wisdom and experience we gained from some of our toughest days. *What we believe about God will help lead us through our hurt from the people of God.*

Believe in God's perfection. The word we use to describe His perfection is *holy*. It means God has never sinned. He has a perfect track record in His dealings with me and every other human throughout history. We, on the other hand, are not perfect. So, when we're part of church, people will wrong us.

When we're hurt or let down by church, it's tempting to try to find healing and peace apart from God and His people.

Sometimes we have the tendency to give up on God when His people let us down. It really should be the opposite. When we see people's imperfection on display, it only highlights God's perfection. And when we put our focus there, it helps us trust Him and continue to obey Him no matter what others might do to us.

Believe in God's presence. There are many amazing verses that tell us why it matters that God is with us. My personal favorite is Psalm 23, where God is compared to a shepherd leading us to a place of protection and peace. A place where we lack nothing—even though we walk through the valley of shadow of death—or in the presence of our enemies.

Other psalms describe God as our fortress and deliverer. Do we believe that God's presence with us makes any difference when we face trouble with people at church?

Psalm 23 helped me through some of my darkest days. I experienced the power of His peace when my anxiety was out of control. I watched Him protect me when I was vulnerable and unable to help myself. I was relieved as He restored my soul, just like the psalm said the Good Shepherd would.

When we're hurt or let down by church, it's tempting to try to find healing and peace apart from God and His people. We look for comfort and relief in all sorts of places, when all we need is actually found right in His presence.

Believe in God's purpose for pain. God uses our pain to grow us. We see that with so many guys in the Bible. (Seriously, take a minute to think about it. Which of them didn't have pain/trials/discouragement?)

God uses our pain to help us rely on Him and to change us to be more like Him. Those are good things, even if it's painful to get there.

When we believe God has purpose for our pain, it helps us trust Him to take us through it. Believing in God's purpose helps us focus on the good He wants to do in our hearts instead of the bitterness we'd rather hold on to.

Believe in God's purpose for church. When someone sins against us, we don't get a pass to abandon the body of Christ. Now, God might have us leave the local church we're part of, only to quickly immerse ourselves in a new church. But we never abandon the people of God as a whole.

■ ■ ■

Tim: How do we know when it's time to go? Leaving a church isn't something we do lightly. But sometimes to get away from believers or leaders who are manipulating, controlling, abusive, bad influences on us, or who are taking the church in a direction we can't support—we have to go. When we've been hurt by people in our church, we desperately need to stay close to God. We need His help to get us through this. And we need His people too . . . just *different* people. As men, we don't leave a church and wander aimlessly for weeks or months without a new church home. And we don't go about the search in a casual way or opt to stay home and cherry-pick from an endless selection of online services. We ask God to help us, and we put our dedicated efforts into finding that new church home *fast,* for our own good, protection, and for the others we'll meet there.

■ ■ ■

As hard as it is to commit to a group of flawed people, we do it because that's what God did with us. We sin against God all the time, and He stays faithful and in a relationship with us. He wants our commitment with the church to look the same.

How Do I Find a New Church When I'm Out on My Own?

To me (Mark), the story is all too familiar. You might have seen this happen with a friend, or maybe it's been your own experience.

It goes like this: Someone moves away to college or starts a new job away from home. Their life gets packed into a car, and they arrive in a new environment with a million details and decisions to figure out. Class schedules, new friend groups, work schedule, dorm room décor, finding the best local coffee shop . . . all the essentials.

What tends to be the final piece put into place? Church. Many will make this the last priority of their move—and some won't ever get around to it.

Sure, people have their reasons, and some of them seem legit. The scary thing is that their reasons become excuses that keep them from what should be a top priority. The best way to get settled in a new church? Develop a plan we commit to *before* we ever pack the car and leave the church we're attending now.

Seven Steps to finding a new church:

Don't do it alone: Ask a pastor, mentor, or solid friend to join the process with you. This will help you avoid the temptation to give up—and to validate your own excuses for doing so. This person will walk with you through each of the following steps, helping you discern which churches are an option and which aren't. This step should be done before you leave the church you're attending.

Make a list: Do some research and put together a list of all potential churches. This step is done before you leave too. A quick Google search will give you a pretty good idea of what's in the area.

In order to make your list, a church needs to fit one major criteria: It must be theologically in line with Christian beliefs. A church will usually have a statement of faith. This is everything they believe about all the major elements of our faith. You can typically find this on their website. Check it out and see if it lines up with your current church.

Before you leave home, pick which church you'll check out on your first weekend. If we don't start on week one, it will only get easier to put off. When you get to where you're going, you'll probably add more churches to the list just based off where others you meet attend.

Limit your preferences and look for the essentials: This new church doesn't need to be just like your last church. Their worship music doesn't need to be a certain style and their preacher doesn't need to remind you of your pastor back home. Holding on to our preferences too tightly makes it nearly impossible to find a new church. Stay focused on the essentials.

Is the Bible taught accurately?

Are there ways for you to use your gifting and serve within the church?

Will you receive the encouragement and accountability from their community to help you keep growing?

Be more curious than critical: We aren't putting the church through a rigorous test each week. If our mind is constantly critiquing the elements of the service—or the people we meet—it will be really tough to evaluate it fairly. Let's commit instead to a more curious approach. We aren't judging every aspect of the church as much as we're trying to understand them. This will involve asking good questions of their people and leaders. Get to know more about the ministries you're passionate about. Yes, this will require taking initiative, but these conversations will help you form a better idea if the church is a good fit for you.

Give it a few weeks: The only exception to this step is if the church doesn't hit the mark on one of the essentials.

If you see that on week one, it's easy to make the decision not to go back. But in most other situations, it'll take a few weeks to make a fair assessment of the church.

Don't fall in love with the hunt: This is where so many get stuck. It can sound super spiritual to say you haven't found the right church yet. Like you're taking the process more seriously if you take longer doing it. I knew guys who spent years "looking." They made it seem like the problem was with every church they attended, but I think it was more an issue of them being too picky. The church will not be perfect. None are. At some point we need to make the decision to jump in and commit to receive all the good the church has to offer, even with the weaknesses that are surely there.

Get involved: You aren't really part of the body until you step into a role. Find a spot to serve, no matter the sacrifice. I know, I know . . . you have classes and deadlines and work, but none of that is too much to stop you from serving in some way.

■ ■ ■

Tim: Finding a new church is a little like buying a used car. They all have dings and scratches. You want one with a good motor—which is that theology element Mark was talking about. You need that church—soon. That church will be like a car in some ways, taking you places as a Christian man—faster than you'd ever get on your own.

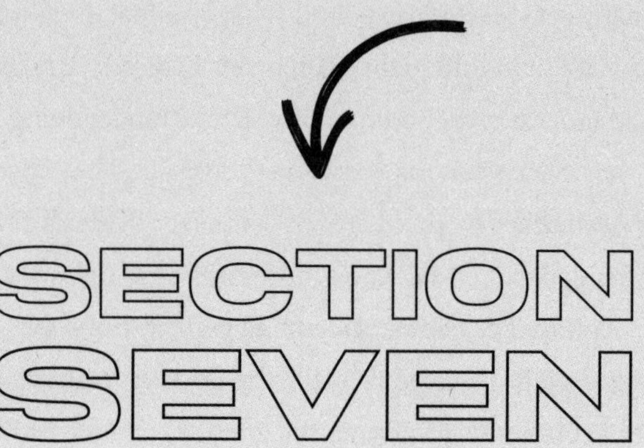

SECTION SEVEN

GOD

There are a number of elements that come into play in our relationship with God. Loving God, for sure. Talking to Him. Being faithful to God. Learning to trust God. Putting His Word into practice.

But what about *fearing* God? Does that have a place in our life as Christian men? Or is that something that should disappear once we put our faith in Jesus?

Fear sounds bad, but it has an essential place in our relationship with God.

I (Tim) can recount at least five times in my life when I've felt there was some unseen, unspeakable evil very near to me . . . at that very moment.

Once was in the Florida Everglades. I was alone, doing research for a novel, and was up over my knees in the dark water of the Glades. The area had a very dark history. Mob killings. Mass murders. There were people who'd traveled to the area and were never seen again. And of course there were the alligators. Venomous snakes.

A sense that I needed to leave twisted my stomach and tightened its grip. I couldn't shake the feeling that if I stayed out there in the wilds any longer, something horrible would happen. Something evil was there. Waiting.

Get out. Get out. Those words looped in my head. Was it my own thoughts? Maybe. But in my heart, at that moment I believed the Lord was impressing that thought on me.

Decision made. I wouldn't go one step deeper into the Everglades. I had to get out—and right now.

Sometimes fear is good. Sometimes bad. But God used fear in a good way that day. I paid attention and am alive today to tell the story. And in our relationship with God, sometimes a healthy *fear* of Him is just the thing to keep us out of danger—and on the right paths.

36

What Does It Really Mean to Fear God in a Healthy Way? And How Will I Be a Better Man for Doing That?

Before entering the promised land, Joshua addressed the people and shared the message he'd received from the Lord.

"Now therefore fear the LORD and serve him in sincerity and in faithfulness" (Joshua 24:14a).

An element of fearing God is foundational to serving him. The book of Proverbs has many, many references to the importance and benefits of fearing the Lord.

"The fear of the LORD is the beginning of wisdom" (Proverbs 9:10a).

But isn't fear of the Lord just an Old Testament thing? Actually, it's a huge part of the New Testament. Jesus Himself made that clear.

"And do not fear those who kill the body but cannot kill the soul. Rather fear him who can destroy both soul and body in hell" (Matthew 10:28).

Fear of God drives us to the cross. But what about this next verse? "There is no fear in love, but perfect love casts out fear. For fear has to do with punishment, and whoever fears has not been perfected in love" (1 John 4:18).

Does this suggest that after putting our faith in Jesus, we no longer should fear God in any way—because of His love for us—and ours for Him?

Not exactly. Let me explain.

In a huge sense, putting our faith in God dissolves our greatest fears.

> **Fear of man.** What can man do to us? Sure, a man could kill us—which simply thrusts us into eternal life with Jesus.
>
> **Fear of death.** Because through Jesus' great love, death has been conquered and can have no permanent hold on us.
>
> **Fear of hell.** God's perfect love has saved us from eternal punishment.

God's love frees us from the *scariest* fears that haunt mankind—which is amazing. Yet, in our ongoing relationship with God, a different type of fearing Him must be part of our life. Check out this verse where God summarizes key characteristics of the early believers:

"So the church throughout all Judea and Galilee and Samaria had peace and was being built up. And walking in the **fear of the Lord** and in the comfort of the Holy Spirit, it multiplied" (Acts 9:31).

I'm married—and my wife's love for me (Tim)—and mine for her—causes me to be careful. There are things I don't do. Places I won't go. Things I won't say. Why? Any of those could damage what we have together. Am I afraid of my wife? Not exactly. But there is a fear. A knowledge that I could easily hurt that relationship. I have it too good to let that happen.

Similarly with God, our relationship with Him is too good for us to get sloppy. I can't live in ways that go against what the Bible teaches and expect God to smile on my life with an "aw shucks, he's only human" attitude. God is just. He must deal with sin—and He has the power to do that. It's easy to say how much we love Him. But do we love Him enough to be careful . . . because we fear distancing ourselves from Him?

I believe this is a huge problem with the church today . . . a lack of the fear of God. We remember His grace. He is good. But we must also remember that He is *just.* He can't excuse our sin.

I desperately need the Lord, *daily.* I need His guidance. His encouragement. His blessing on my life. I need His peace. His wisdom. If I get sloppy with how I live out my faith . . . if I disobey His Word or quench His Spirit, how can I expect God to bless me in any of those ways? If I don't stay connected to Jesus, the Vine, how can I expect Him to bless me with the fruit of His Spirit? God is just, and He disciplines us when we stray. I love God—and also fear the "just" side of Him and the consequences of distancing myself from Him. Love and fear work together to make me the man God wants me to be.

Yes, because of what Jesus did for me on the cross, He has ultimately saved me from the eternal punishment I deserve. He has extended massive grace to us. And He continues to give us grace in countless ways. But that doesn't give me a pass to get sloppy with how I live . . . with how I obey Him. Paul warns us in Romans 6 that God's grace isn't a license to keep on sinning. I don't want to deliberately put myself in a position where God needs to discipline me. I'm too grateful for the grace He's given me to do that. I want to be the man God has designed me to be.

God, who does not change, said this:

"Oh that they had such a heart as this always, to fear me and to

Countless times, healthy fear of the God I love—and who loves me—has kept me on the right paths—or gotten me off wrong ones.

keep all my commandments, that it might go well with them and with their descendants forever!" (Deuteronomy 5:29).

Clearly, because of God's great love for us, He desires us to have a healthy fear that keeps us close to Him. Then we find that He blesses us in ways we'd likely only experience when we're staying close to Him. A truly "God-fearing" man seems to be extremely rare. Fearing God may be largely missing in the church, but let's not let it be missing from our lives as men.

Countless times, healthy fear of the God I love—and who loves me—has kept me on the right paths—or gotten me off wrong ones. "The fear of the LORD is a fountain of life, that one may turn away from the snares of death" (Proverbs 14:27).

Thank God for that kind of fear!

As men, sometimes we take paths that distance us from God—which is a scarier place to be than when I was alone in the Everglades. Let's open our eyes. See that we're in danger of messing things up for good. Let's confess our sin and change our direction fast—with His help. Better yet, let that fear of God keep us from ever going someplace we shouldn't.

■ ■ ■

Mark: ***How can we grow in our fear of God?*** *Pay attention to the results of people's sin.* It could be consequences they face—or lack of satisfaction they receive from their sin. All of it promotes a healthy fear of God in our heart. It's what happened in the early church when God struck Ananias and Sapphira down for their sin (Acts 5:11). I've watched God unravel men's lives because of their sin, and I keep their example in view to keep my fear of God strong.

Ask God to grow your fear of Him. I prayed this almost every day for a year, and it was amazing the ways God brought new understanding for what it meant to fear God in my life.

What Does It Look Like to Love God Today?

Imagine your best friend, Finn, is totally in love with a girl named Georgia. She's quick to tell you how much she loves Finn too. More than once you've seen Georgia sing love songs to Finn, right out loud—even when others are around. One time you actually saw tears trickling down her cheeks as she sang about how she loves Finn more than anybody in the world.

But as time goes on, you notice she doesn't return his calls as she once did. It's like there are times Georgia goes totally off-grid. Days later she'll call him back, always making some lame excuse about how she'd been too tired, busy, or just forgot to call back.

But most disturbing? You've caught her lying to him. She tells Finn she's going to do one thing but does another. When the truth comes out, Georgia promises never to do it again. But she does. You realize she's living a double life. One as his devoted girlfriend, and the other where her one true love seems to be herself. Georgia recently accused Finn of being distant. You know better. If she feels distance, it's only because she doesn't stay close.

That's definitely *not* the kind of love I'm (Tim) interested in—and I'm pretty sure you aren't either. But sometimes that's exactly how we treat God.

Loving God isn't just about singing songs to Him in a worship service—or telling others how much you love Him. Loving God is about *obeying* him. If we don't value God enough to do what He says, we can't say we love Him.

"For this is the love of God, that we keep his commandments. And his commandments are not burdensome" (1 John 5:3).

Makes sense, doesn't it? To love someone isn't just saying the words "I love you."

"Little children, let us not love in word or talk but in deed and in truth" (1 John 3:18).

Our love for someone is often shown by the things that we do—or avoid doing—because of our love. God wants us to show our love to Him by obeying Him and loving others.

"If anyone says, 'I love God,' and hates his brother, he is a liar; for he who does not love his brother whom he has seen cannot love God whom he has not seen" (1 John 4:20).

If we want to be the kind of man God designed us to be, let's love God enough to obey His Word. That isn't always easy. Remember the Foundational Five. God can help give us a heart to love Him and others *more,* if we ask. Here's a secret. As we look back and remember all He's done for us—or forward to see in faith all He's planned for us—it becomes easier and easier to love Him and others the way we should.

That's so true, growing stronger in the Foundational Five will have a direct impact on the way we obey God. I know, I know . . . that part of the book was a long time ago, but it is called the foundation for a reason! Those five things are what we stand on to take every step in becoming the man God wants us to be. **—Mark**

How Can I Follow a God Who Allows Bad Things to Happen to Good People?

God can stop natural disasters. He can cure any disease. He could stop human trafficking. He can stop any evil if He wanted to. Why doesn't He? Someone might challenge us with something like this: "If this is God's world, why does He allow horrible things to happen? I've got no interest in following a God like that—and I can't see why you would, either."

> **First, realize that *technically* this is God's world,** but it's been given to the devil on loan right now. When sin entered the world, the world became the temporary domain for the devil and his demons. That's how the devil could offer the world back to Jesus in Luke 4:5–7:
>
> > "The devil took him up and showed him all the kingdoms of the world in a moment of time, and said to him, 'To you I will give all this authority

> and their glory, for it has been delivered to me, and I give it to whom I will. If you, then, will worship me, it will all be yours.'"

Yeah, the world is a mess. That's what happens when the *devil* is on the throne of the world—not God.

And God *did* do something to fix the world—for good—when He gave His son to die for the lost and deceived. He offers us heaven, where the devil has no corrupting influence. And someday He will make all things new. But in His mercy, He waits until every last one who is to be saved puts their faith in Jesus.

"The Lord is not slow to fulfill his promise as some count slowness, but is patient toward you, not wishing that any should perish, but that all should reach repentance" (2 Peter 3:9).

There are other reasons God allows bad things to happen. I (Tim) jotted down five here—and likely you could add more to the list.

1. Sometimes bad things push people to seek and find God.
2. Sometimes the bad things drive Christians closer to God. That's a good thing.
3. Sometimes He uses bad things to nudge us into changing directions. To get us off wrong or dangerous paths and onto His path for us.

4. Sometimes bad things cause us to have more compassion for others or prepare us to help others through hard things in their life.

5. Sometimes bad things seem to break us . . . but it's only then that He can shine through us like He never did before.

But still . . . some of the things that happen to innocent kids and to decent people are incredibly tragic. Does God see? Does He care? Why doesn't He step in?

We know He sees. The Bible makes that clear. He doesn't miss a thing. He sees the evil. The injustice. For those who do evil and hurt others in so many ways, there will be a day of reckoning. A judgment day where they stand before God and justice will be served. Romans 12:19 reminds us of this. "Beloved, never avenge yourselves, but leave it to the wrath of God, for it is written 'Vengeance is mine, I will repay, says the Lord.'"

Facing the wrath of God is a terrifying thing.

He understands our pain. Sometimes we think Jesus enjoyed the life of a celebrity. Crowds following Him. People hanging on every word He said. But Isaiah 53 gives a very different picture. It tells us that Jesus was oppressed, despised, and crushed. He endured injustice, sorrow, grief, and pain—physical and emotional. And the Gospels show us that Jesus endured betrayal, loss of friends, bullying, mocking, and all kinds of hardship. Although Jesus is our King, He didn't live like a king when He came to earth. It helps me to know that He has experienced and understands our grief and hurt and pain. And because He understands and cares,

He wants us to bring our pain and cares to Him.

"Cast your burden on the Lord, and he will sustain you; he will never permit the righteous to be moved" (Psalm 55:22).

". . . casting all your anxieties on him, because he cares for you" (1 Peter 5:7).

When you experience hard things, and your heart is broken, bring it to the One who was broken for us. Use that to drive you closer to Him.

Sometimes He does step in. Tsunamis. Earthquakes. Hurricanes. Natural disasters destroy and kill. Innocent people get murdered. Entire families are destroyed because of a drunk driver. Cancer takes out a mom, a grandma, a child. Sometimes when horrible things happen, we may still question why God doesn't *do* something. But the truth is, there are countless times He helps us in our hour of need.

I ran a family business that was struggling. Honestly, it got to the point where I felt the situation was going to kill me. I prayed for God to bless it and bring in the opportunities I needed to stay afloat. I knew He could do that—easy. And many times, He answered that prayer by giving me a little extra business that week so I could get by. He helped me over and over as I struggled, so I knew He was beside me. "Even though I walk through the valley of the shadow of death, I will fear no evil, for you are with me" (Psalm 23:4).

But the business was still going down, and in the end, we had to close. I learned that He hadn't abandoned me. Through the hard things and the grief, He kept me close to Him. He was changing me and making me into a better man—the one He'd designed me to be. And He redirected me into a whole new occupation that was part of His plan for me. He *had* stepped in to answer my prayers . . . but differently than I'd expected.

Yeah, a lot of bad, bad things happen in this world. We understand that God in many ways is letting the effects of sin play out to their natural consequences. For now. And we know He provided a plan to rescue us from sin and its consequences. And sometimes He gives us those little boosts. A person walks away from what should have been a fatal car accident. Somebody survives a natural disaster, stunning everyone who hears their story. A mom survives cancer. Some call these events miracles. I like to think of them as reminders—that God is still there. That someday He'll put an end to all the pain and suffering and injustice and grief. Someday, He'll wipe every tear away. And maybe that's when we'll really understand why He didn't step in more than we really hoped He would. Maybe that will be the moment when we'll fully realize how much He actually did.

A lot of bad, bad things happen in this world. God in many ways is letting the effects of sin play out to their natural consequences. For now.

SECTION
EIGHT

TECHNOLOGY

I (Mark) live with a bit of self-denial about how long ago I graduated college. In my mind, it was a handful of years . . . five or so. It really doesn't feel like my college experience was so far back, until I refer to the technology I used at the time.

When I was in college . . .

I showed up with a desktop computer.

It was the first time I had a cellphone that wasn't shared with my mom.

My friends and I used MapQuest to get around.

The first iPhone came out while I was there.

I didn't know what an app was.

The list could go on. What was once pretty high-tech stuff now feels antiquated and irrelevant. That's sort of the narrative of technology, isn't it? What's shiny and new now is outdated and replaceable in a matter of months—or a couple of short years.

Technology changes the way we do business, the way we socialize, the way we drive, learn, focus, sleep, organize, relax, create, and communicate. It impacts the way we see our world and how we live in it.

Tech changes happen so quickly that we don't always notice how it shapes our habits . . . our life. But at what cost? Are we better or worse disciples of Jesus with a phone in our pocket?

As I look back at the years since graduating college, I'm truly grateful for some improvements to technology and the ways they help my everyday life. But I wonder if what is convenient and fast is simultaneously working against some of the slow and steady work God wants to form in me over the course of a lifetime.

How Do I Use Technology Without Getting Swallowed Up By It?

I (Mark) don't think I'm alone when I say I've seen the way technology can take over and consume my day and my focus and my desires. People in the secular realm are paying more attention to the negative effect this is having on our mental health. But what about spiritually?

Have you seen your phone help or hurt your growth in the Foundational Five? For me, it's been a battle in each area.

As I scroll other people's lives as posted on social media, I grow discontent in the God-given purpose of mine.

The more time I spend on the phone, the more my desire grows for the quick comfort and dopamine rush that a phone can bring. "Somebody liked my post . . . actually lots of people did!" That leads right to a level of addiction. It's hard to live a life of self-control when I let my phone control me.

- When I let my phone into every crevice of free time in my day, I am far less likely to hear the quiet conviction and prompting of the Holy Spirit.
- My time with God is often distracted by the desire to check my phone, respond to texts, or immerse my mind in "something easy." This is the opposite of "abiding in Christ."
- As I immerse myself in my phone and the social media world, my desires begin to be shaped by what I read and see *there* instead of by the truth in God's Word.

This is impacting all of us spiritually. It can stunt our growth or sidetrack us from what's important. It's essential that we don't allow technology to be our master.

A phone is like a chainsaw. A really great tool, but dangerous if we don't control it. Phones have evolved to the point where they're not so much communication devices as they are control devices. *Phones can influence what you think. What you buy. How you spend your time. How you relate to others.* Our phones can become our master in all those areas. As men, let's fight against that! Use the tool, but don't become its tool. **—Tim**

Here are five habits I've implemented (with varying consistency) in my life. I find that when I am doing these things well, technology doesn't have the same stranglehold on my heart and focus.

Phone is never first: Get into your morning routine (coffee/Bible/prayer) before using your phone. (This includes middle of the night social media scrolling.) When I turn to my phone first, I'll turn to it more frequently during the day.

Establish dead zones: Set times and places where your phone isn't allowed (dinner table, an hour before bed, bathroom, within easy reach while you drive). My favorite and most important dead zone? From the start of dinner until after my kids are in bed.

Normalize phoneless moments: Practice leaving your phone behind. You don't need it at the restaurant, when you run inside a store, or as you walk around your house or apartment. When you leave your phone behind, you'll likely experience phantom rings and moments when you make an empty pocket grab! It's like going through withdrawal, which ought to tell us something right there.

Phones open the entire world to us—and blind us to whatever is right in front of us.

Sabbath shutdown: Once a week I try to have a full stop in my work as I rest/delight/worship. Coupling that discipline to Sabbath with the habit of turning my phone off for the day has been life changing. Honest confession: Every time I turn my phone off for the day, I have a period of irritation—highlighting my addiction and desire to find distraction and comfort in my phone.

Delete social media apps: If you want to scroll on social media, you'll either have to use a browser or go through the app store. Tedious I know; but this can help you avoid the quick scroll while in line at the store or any other spare eleven seconds you find in your day.

■ ■ ■

Tim: *But I'm afraid I'll miss something if I don't have my phone.* We can feel that way, right? We might miss a text. Funny posts. Glimpses of what our friends are up to. But the truth is we often miss *so much more* when we're checking our phone. We've all seen parents so absorbed in their phone that they're oblivious to their kids who are dying for attention. We've seen friends get so mesmerized with their phone that they miss moments and conversation with the others at the table with them. We've all had a close call while driving because we glanced at our phone or pecked out a text. Phones open the entire world to us—and blind us to whatever is right in front of us. Giving our phones less real estate in our life may cause us to miss a few things, sure . . . but we'll gain so much more.

40

Am I Addicted to My Phone?

Yes.

Well, that might have been the easiest question I (Mark) answer.

But really, you are. We all are. If there was any doubt, how about we ask Google? A quick search shows these as the common signs of addiction:

You look at your phone while doing mundane daily tasks (bathroom, walking, working) or at the first sign of waiting (stop light, microwave, line at the store). Are any of us still wondering if we're addicted? Consider:

You feel compelled to check your phone during other activities, like a movie or a meal.

You have trouble completing tasks.

You have trouble sleeping.

Other signs of addiction?

A lot of us admit we're addicted. But why does an addiction to phones matter? It's so easy to normalize what we see happening to our own hearts because we see it all around us. We all relate to the late-night doomscrolling. Everyone is on their phones in the spare moments of their day. What has become common is too often confused as harmless. When you think about it, an addiction like this goes directly against what it means to be a follower of Jesus.

> ***An addiction*** *becomes our desire in ways that should be reserved for God.* Our phone is taking more than just minutes of our day—it's grabbing a position in our heart. Throughout the Bible, we're reminded to love God with all of our heart. To love God is to make Him most important in our day. Phone addiction works against that. As we spend more time with our phone, we *want* more time with our phone. It gets hard to focus on most anything else—including during our time with God. Our love for checking that text, replying to that email, and scrolling through that app has surpassed any casual fondness. Our urge to check our phone—even during our time with God—is a litmus test of what we desire most.
>
> ***An addiction*** *becomes our master in ways reserved for God.* Think about the ways our phone has changed us over time. Our habits, thinking, attitudes, and actions have changed. An addiction becomes our master and forms us into its own image and its own purpose for our life. These are all things we're supposed to be

getting from God. He is supposed to guide us into forming good habits. He is the master who changes our heart so that we can live out His purposes over our lifetime. When we let an addiction control our actions and thoughts, we also invite it to change us. Only God should have that power and influence in our life.

***An addiction** becomes our source for comfort in ways reserved for God.* I can't count the number of times I turned to a screen to provide refuge and peace in the uncomfortable/difficult moments of this past week. A difficult email, a hard conversation, awkward silence, tough parenting moment, stuck on a project . . . all of these moments became opportunities to pull out my phone to find sweet relief. The regularity of this has made it clear: My discipline to find these things in God has taken a back seat to the reflex I now have to find it in my phone.

■ ■ ■

Tim: Our addictions keep us from obeying God's two greatest commandments. In Matthew 22, Jesus talks about the big two. Loving God. Loving others. Mark just talked about how our addiction to phones can overshadow our love for God. It does the same when it comes to loving others. Phones cause us to miss opportunities to see others around us who may be in need or hurting. Unless we beat this addiction, we'll have a hard time fulfilling God's two greatest commandments.

■ ■ ■

My (Mark) heart feels far from David's, who wrote in Psalm 62:5–7:

"For God alone, O my soul, wait in silence, for my hope is from him. He only is my rock and my salvation, my fortress; I shall not be shaken. On God rests my salvation and glory; my mighty rock, my refuge is God."

The more I embrace my addiction to devices, the less my heart resembles David's. Putting down our devices is more than a good decision for our mental health. It's a step in the right direction on the path of following Jesus—and growing to be more like Him.

How do I beat my phone addiction? Go back to the Foundational Five. Self-control and Holy Spirit-control are essential to set new boundaries–and to keep them. **–Tim**

41

How Can the Way I Use Technology Help—or Hurt—My Relationship with God?

I (Mark) just spent some time looking up quotes on technology. Who doesn't love a catchy line from some famous person, right? I'd hoped to find something that spoke to the way technology has made our world more accessible. But after scrolling online for ten minutes, I didn't find anything I liked.

Then it hit me. My Google search underscored the point I was hoping to make with the quote. I was able to access and sift through lists of obscure and random quotes in a matter of minutes. This is a small example we see on a huge scale every day.

Think about it; as technology advances, our access also increases. Europe is accessible by plane in a way it wasn't two hundred years ago. The skills to tackle a home project can be learned from accessing any one of the hundreds of how-to videos on YouTube. We have access to news 24/7—and access to the world leaders making the headlines through their personal Instagram or X accounts. People are more accessible . . . places are more accessible . . . information is more accessible.

We tend to focus on the ways this can hurt us spiritually—because it certainly can. But we find productive ways to utilize new opportunities technology brings with our schooling, jobs, hobbies, entertainment, and travel. Are there ways we can use that extra access technology offers to benefit our relationship with God?

Colossians 3 fits well into this conversation. I still remember when I read it for the first time. I was in high school, and it was like verse 2 jumped off the page. "Set your minds on things that are above, not on things that are on earth." This verse is one of a handful that changed my life at the time. It became a daily pursuit of mine to set my mind on God.

This is often the struggle with technology, isn't it? It has such power over what we think about and focus on. It often thrusts us toward a self-focused/distracted/consumer life. It would seem as though technology is only capable of pushing us further from a mind focused on "things that are above."

But the truth is, technology also gives us access to resources that will help us live out Colossians 3:2.

> ***Worship music*** *is more accessible.* We used to have to buy CDs and were limited to listening to them on a player at home or in our car. Now we can stream thousands of bands and songs with one subscription. And we carry it around with us in our pocket. We can put worship music on at any point of our day.
>
> ***Biblical knowledge*** *is more accessible.* We have access to a seemingly endless supply of content. Sermons, podcasts, and audiobooks are all easily accessible to listen to throughout our day. I've watched men grow leaps and bounds in their walk with God because they started listening to Bible teaching throughout their week.
>
> ***The Bible*** *is more accessible.* Bible apps are so helpful. They offer daily plans for Bible reading, tools to help you do more in depth study of the Word, and some audio options that make the text super interactive.

On your drive to your job or school, during your workout, while you work you have the opportunity to use technology to help you set your mind on God. We have access now that believers never had before. How can we use that more to our benefit than we already are?

▪ ▪ ▪

Tim: A car is another example of amazing technology. It allows us to go farther—faster. But a car can also hurt us and others if we don't use it right. And we certainly don't take our car everywhere. Sometimes we walk or bike. We park our car outside or in the garage at night. We don't rip out walls so we can bring our car into our bedroom. Let's apply that same sense of healthy balance with our phones, screens, and other technology too. Absolutely, let's use phones or screens to help us or others in ways that align with God's purposes. But let's also keep some healthy walls in place. In other words, know when to leave technology parked outside.

■ ■ ■

It's interesting, within this heading of "technology" we've warned against the danger of being consumed and addicted to our phones, and we've also encouraged you to fully maximize the access we're given with them. How do we pursue the one without getting caught up in the other? The answer to that is found back in our Foundational Five. While every one of them applies here, I think "self-control" is the most helpful. As we grow in self-control, we set ourselves up to build good habits with technology and reinforce the boundary walls to guard us against what could destroy us.

SECTION
NINE

SPIRITUAL LIFE

My (Mark) extended family decided it was time we all got together for a reunion. The idea at surface level was great. My issue was more in the details.

Date: June 23

Location: Phoenix, Arizona

Really? Phoenix? In the summer? Who plans a reunion in the desert? It's common for temperatures to hover uncomfortably over 100 degrees that time of year. But it's a dry heat, right?

Arizona in the summer lived up to everything I'd dreaded. Words like "hot" and "sunny" don't do it justice. The words I'd go with? *Smoldering, roasting,* and *blazing*. All of this, with zero clouds in the sky as far as the eye could see. No relief in sight.

We went through water bottles like my kids go through fruit snacks. I was managing sunburn after about twelve hours of boots on the ground. The swimming pool was warm—and about as refreshing as piping hot tea would be to a marathon runner.

You get the picture. It was survival mode. And all of that . . . with two young kids who just wanted to ride horses.

At some point someone suggested that we go to Sedona, a two-hour journey north into the mountains. The mountains! Out of the valley, and into temperatures that dropped by 15–20 degrees during the day and down to a soothing 56 degrees at night. Literal chills. It didn't take much convincing to get the full crew on board. We were all in, desperate and determined to get out of the valley heat.

If you've been following Jesus for a year—or a decade—I'm nearly certain you've had a time when your relationship with God felt like a desert.

Dry.

Dead.

Survival mode.

No relief in sight.

These are the times your walk with God lacks life. You aren't the tree bearing fruit in John 15. You feel more like you're withering. You aren't the Psalm 1 tree with roots deeply planted alongside a stream. You're a tumbleweed blowing across the gravel road. Green pastures? More like dry, sand-caked dirt.

You've been there? Me too.

It's in those moments we need the same urgency and desperation to get out of our spiritual desert as my family did to escape the physical desert. Once we recognize that, we've taken the first step out. But it's what we do next that'll make the real difference.

My Spiritual Life Is Dry. How Do I Escape the Desert?

Spiritual dryness won't go away by itself. Like me (Mark) taking my family to the mountains, we have to make a move to escape the spiritual dryness. That takes effort on our part.

The weirdest thing about the spiritual desert? We make it so normal to hang out there. We get comfortable. We feel exhausted and totally burned out, yet we often choose to stay in that place. So, we trudge on, sunburned and thirsty, unsure of how to get to the sweet relief of Sedona.

Even great men of God run out of gas. We read of it in the Bible, and I see it often in men around me. Spiritual dryness leads to discouragement, fear, cynicism, and a distorted view of life. We lose hope and vision. Spiritual deserts are dangerous places! **—Tim**

It's strange, right? Things die in the desert. If you're there, you should be thinking about how to get out. Instead, often we focus on growing our abilities, portfolio, experiences, and following—thinking that'll satisfy us, even though they're all things our soul doesn't need.

David gives us an example to follow, one that's helped me many times.

"O God you are my God: earnestly I seek you; my soul thirsts for you; my flesh faints for you, as in a dry and weary land where there is no water" (Psalm 63:1).

David talks about seeking God earnestly. There's a sincerity, a desperation, and a longing for what God can give him. He knows that God satisfies in ways that no job, relationship, or personal achievement can. He celebrates that in verse 5—and this is the good news for anyone in the desert right now:

"My soul will be satisfied as with fat and rich food, and my mouth will praise you with joyful lips" (Psalm 63:5).

You see that? There *is* relief for us. It was with God all along. God can and will bring life to you. As dry as you feel, and as dead as your relationship might seem . . . God can bring life there.

So how does that look exactly, to seek God earnestly? What does it mean to thirst for Him?

Desperation.

You don't just casually try to find your way out of the harsh elements. The desert is a place of death and we're in a desperate search for relief. Just like my family aggressively chased cool temperatures two hours north, we need to seek refreshment in God's presence, with desperation, no matter what we need to sacrifice to get there.

In Psalm 63, David says he "earnestly" seeks. He knew the importance of placing priority on finding satisfaction in God. In Romans 12:11, Paul warns against being "slothful," and encourages us to have "zeal." I love the tenacity and aggressiveness of that. If we think we'll get out of our spiritual desert with a lazy/slothful/mosey-along pace in our pursuit of Jesus, we're somehow missing the cues of how deadly and dangerous the desert truly is.

Our spiritual desert highlights a deep desire for God and a desperate need to pursue Him as our way out.

So which way to Sedona? How do I seek God and escape the spiritually dry phase I'm in? Here are some practices I've found helpful.

Remind yourself of spiritually rich times. This is a reality check to see how far away I am from where I want or used to be. Imagine it like this: You're at your house about to eat a hot dog you just pulled from the pot of boiling water. You don't have a bun, so you just stick it on a piece of bread. To make matters worse you don't have any condiments in your fridge, but you're hungry, so you take a bite. And while chewing you remind yourself of better days . . . that Chicago-style hot dog . . . loaded with everything on it.

You've tasted and experienced His goodness before. Remind yourself of those days . . . and let that help give you the drive to get back to where you want to be.

Go back to what's familiar. There are a handful of verses and passages that I regularly go back to because I love them so much. If you're in a dry season, try taking a break from the reading plan you're on and go back to a passage that tends to fire you up or that you have gleaned a lot from in the past.

Make a plan you can keep. The temptation is to overcommit and set a rigorous Bible-reading plan in motion to make sure you get back on track. What often happens is a week of great progress followed up by lack of follow-through. If you're in the desert, you probably can't handle too much too quickly. You won't get out of the desert by sprinting for three days or a week. Instead, give yourself steps you know you can do, and make those a habit for the next couple of months.

Make a plan you'll enjoy. Getting out of the desert should be enjoyable! Think about all the ways you can be with God that you'd find pleasure in and build those into habits within your day. I love making worship song playlists on Spotify and listening to them as I take a jog through my neighborhood. Guess what, that counts as time with God, plus it was so enjoyable! Another thing that I love is coffee. It turns out coffee pairs great with Bible reading. God and I hang out over a cup of coffee every morning. How can you mix things that you love—with spending time with God?

Pray for what you need. In Philippians 1:11, Paul prays for righteous fruit. He knows he can't just grow spiritually stronger on his own. He asks God to do that in his life for him. Let's pray for God to grow and strengthen us spiritually.

▪ ▪ ▪

Tim: Here's a few more things that may help you get free from spiritual dryness.

Rest. Sometimes I feel spiritually parched because I'm exhausted. Maybe we need a good night's sleep. Or maybe we need a real change of routine—like getting away for a couple of days to a lake or vacation spot.

Reset. Like rebooting a computer, sometimes we need to go back to our Christian default settings. Reread the *Hard Emotions* section where we talk about strengthening ourselves in the Lord. It helps to get our focus on the God we serve, and off how we feel.

Reflect. Are there things in our life that don't belong there? Sin has a way of drying us up. Pride, selfishness, unforgiveness, bitterness, hypocrisy, pornography, hard heart. We need to confess and turn from sin.

Reach out. Serving at church or doing things for others takes our mind off ourselves. Sometimes that joy of doing for others is enough to get us on our way out of the desert.

■ ■ ■

We did get to Sedona, and it was amazing! A highlight from that day? Swimming with my daughter at a place called Slide Rock. Cold water rushing through the canyon . . . so refreshing! Such a difference from just a day earlier in the extreme heat. In that moment, you think I missed the desert? Not a chance. I'd found a place of satisfaction and life, and it was worth every effort to get there.

How Do I Make Sure I Don't Develop a "Hard Heart" Like the Bible Warns Against?

A hard heart can have many devastating effects on us as men. As we begin to understand the consequences of a hard heart, it gives us all the incentive we need to guard ourselves against it. I've

(Tim) seen examples in the Bible of at least nine scary things that can happen if we allow our heart to harden.

We make bad decisions. When the Israelites were slaves in Egypt, God sent Moses to Pharoah with a simple message. "Let my people go." God sent horrific plagues over Egypt to help convince Pharoah. Time after time Pharoah refused. He "hardened his heart"—and sometimes God hardened Pharoah's heart too. When our heart is hard, we resist admitting we're wrong. We find it hard to repent. Pharoah kept making bad decisions, such as refusing to free the slaves, with devastating consequences to himself and all Egypt.

We fail to fear God. The plagues described in Exodus proved God was real, powerful, and not to be trifled with. That should've caused Pharoah to fear going against God. But his hard heart drove him to disregard God—and eventually Pharoah lost his firstborn child and his entire army as a result.

We miss God's best for us. Because of their hard hearts, a whole generation of Israelites missed God's rest *and* a new home for them in the promised land. Their hearts were hard, and they failed to trust God with their future. As a result, they were forced back into the desert—for forty years. Numbers 14 tells the tragic story. Hard hearts always lead to deserts for us as men.

We destroy our closest relationships. In Matthew 19:8, Jesus revealed the root cause of divorce going all the way back to the time of Moses: hardness of heart. And in every case that I've seen in my lifetime, I've noticed it still boils down to that same issue. It might be her heart, his heart, or both. But somewhere in the relationship, hard-heartedness caused a couple who once loved each other to death down a path that would kill their marriage.

We lose our compassion. In Mark 3 the Pharisees were furious after Jesus healed a man on the Sabbath. Their hearts were hard, and they had no compassion for the disabled man.

We develop our own code of conduct, push it on others—and enforce it ruthlessly. In the Mark 3 passage mentioned above, Jesus wasn't playing by the Pharisees' rules. Instead of questioning their own standards, the Pharisees stood behind them all the more . . . to their own peril. Can you imagine how we alienate others, miss opportunities, and distance ourselves from God when we become legalistic in our thinking?

We seek to discredit or silence those who don't respect our thinking or actions. After Jesus called them out on their erroneous thinking, Mark 3:6 says the Pharisees strategized how to destroy Him. They used lies, half-truths, and eventually incited others to rally against Him. Don't we see that in our world today? Hard-hearted people seek to silence those who disagree with them.

We grumble against God—and His servants. Numbers 20 tells of how the Israelites complained against Moses, which was really complaining against God. Psalm 95:8 reveals this was due to their hardened hearts.

We miss seeing the hand of God at work around us. This is the danger of a hardened heart that so many miss. Just after feeding five thousand people with five loaves and two fish, Jesus sent the disciples into a boat to cross the sea while He went to pray. Later, the disciples, straining at the oars against a strong headwind, saw Jesus walking on the water to cross the sea Himself. They were terrified, thinking Jesus was a ghost. Surely no living person could do such a thing—it had to be a spirit! But the text explains that they'd missed the significance of the miracle of feeding the five thousand because their hearts were hard. Incredibly, they didn't fully understand they were seeing God at work when Jesus fed the crowd. They didn't quite catch that if He could multiply food like that, He could walk on water.

"And he got into the boat with them, and the wind ceased. And they were utterly astounded, for they did not understand about the loaves, but their hearts were hardened" (Mark 6:51–52).

If we failed to see the hand of God working around us, wouldn't we get discouraged, maybe feel like giving up, or become fearful?

Another word for a hard heart is *stubborn*. If we're stubborn in relationships in our life, chances are we're also stubborn in some ways with God in our spiritual life. One way to avoid a hard heart toward God is to root out stubbornness in your life toward people. **—Mark**

So, how do we keep from getting a hard heart?

> ***Watch for it.*** Do we have one or more of the symptoms above?
>
> ***Ask the Lord* to show us where our heart is hard—and to soften it.**
>
> ***Obey God's leading* without hesitation—even if we're scared.** Stubbornly failing to do this is how the Israelites messed up so badly in Numbers 14.

> ***Avoid doing wrong things.*** Nothing hardens a heart faster than resisting the urging of the Holy Spirit—or failing to put the Word into practice. When we choose to sin—even though we know better, hardening begins. Scary thought, right?

It's no wonder God says so much about the heart in the Bible. Men, let's guard our hearts against hardening. A hard heart impacts every area of our life. This is really, really important.

"Above all else, guard your heart, for everything you do flows from it" (Proverbs 4:23 NIV).

44

I Don't Have Time to Read My Bible. Is There a Way to Change That?

I (Mark) know it seems like you don't have time but trust me . . . if you don't find time now, you won't later.

Let's agree on this: time with God is essential. Which means for us men, it needs to be a priority in our day. Think back to our Foundational Five. We can't build a foundation of biblical manhood if we miss time with God. The reality is, you'll not find a man of God who doesn't spend time with God. So don't make this an option in your day . . . we *must* find time.

Let's think through your schedule together and see where we can find time to be with God.

In college, I spent time with God right after my last class ended. Some friends found gaps in their day between classes or at night before bed to intentionally meet with God. So many options! It just takes some intentionality to block out that time and not let anything else touch it.

But I'll bet I can find more time in your day. This time slot has proven to be the absolute best/most consistent/least distracted/most commonly used time slot for not only myself, but also every single man I look up to.

First thing in the morning.

We can always find time in our schedule here, because we can wake up earlier. There *is* time there . . . it just comes at a sacrifice of sleep. Most mornings you'll have to battle laziness, fatigue, barely cohesive thoughts, and the reflex to silence your alarm. You can win that fight, and you'll find time with God.

Waking up to be with God first thing in the morning is easier said than done. What's helped me? Slowly build the habit. If you start with an intense mentality . . . "*I'm going to wake up at 5:30 and spend an hour with God,*" the habit won't last.

Here's what I recommend. Start small. I'd bet most of us have fifteen minutes in our morning—without waking earlier—if we didn't doomscroll or check emails.

I can almost guarantee that if you stick with fifteen minutes in the morning, something amazing will happen. You'll actually like it—and prefer the morning time slot!

I'll promise you one more thing. At some point, your fifteen minutes will be up—and you'll wish you had more. Now, you're ready to build on the good habit you've started. Give yourself five more minutes the next day. Yeah, you'll have to wake up earlier. But it's easier now because you'll know time with God is worth it.

We talked about ways to connect with God throughout your

day in the Foundational Five section—especially where we talk about abiding, because Christ is enough. It's worth rereading that for some practical ideas. But here's the thing, guys. We *do* have the time to read our Bible daily. Let's find that block of time . . . and you'll find that time you invest is worth it on every level.

SECTION
TEN

OUR CULTURE

5, 4, 3, 2, 1—BLASTOFF! I (Mark) pressed the ignition button and watched the launch pad with anticipation. The engine gave off a loud sizzle before shooting the model rocket hundreds of feet into the air. All eyes tracked the line of smoke streaking into the Arizona sky. Just when it seemed as if we were going to lose our visual, the parachute shot out and the rocket began its descent.

All of us kids took off running, dodging cacti as we raced

through the chalky desert sand, trying to be the first to retrieve the rocket. Sometimes one of us would catch it on the fly, sometimes it got caught in a tree, and some rockets never made it home.

I loved those childhood vacation days spent in that desert with my dad, cousins, and brothers. Shooting off rockets, hiking trails, exploring the wild, always looking for snakes (and never finding one). We got to know the landscape pretty well. The dried-up riverbed. The old rusted-out Plymouth Valiant in the middle of nowhere, abandoned and pockmarked with bullet holes. All of it was so familiar. I can close my eyes and picture everything as if I was there again.

A few years ago, I took my kids to that same desert. I wanted them to experience the place where I'd created so many memories when I was their age. I had the day mapped out, but when we got there, I was surprised that nothing I saw matched what I remembered.

A white brick wall stood where we used to enter the desert. On the other side sat a subdivision of newly built houses. New streets, new stores, and grass everywhere!

The desert was gone. The familiar terrain I grew up exploring had changed into something totally new . . . thanks to thirty years of innovation and progress.

Our culture is a lot like that sliver of earth that morphed into something new. The cultural landscape constantly changes. The way we talk about issues and view various topics looks very different now than back when I was a kid. It will continue to evolve into something a decade from now that none of us would recognize today.

That's the way of culture, I guess. It embraces one thing today, then cancels it tomorrow. It's deeper than just the music or the clothing style of the day. Culture influences how we view ourselves, our purpose, and the way we live our lives. Culture is constantly reshaping the narrative of our day into new terrain.

Here's the thing. While culture is constantly changing what's acceptable—and what's not—that isn't how God operates.

God is the same today as when He formed the earth.

God's words haven't changed.

God's definition of sin is the same.

God's purpose for believers hasn't changed.

Our world looks to create new and evolve, but God doesn't need to. He's already perfect, and entirely true. Our goal is to avoid shifting our views back and forth with our unstable culture. Instead, we aim to follow the teachings of Jesus—which leads us on the same path believers have walked for thousands of years.

If we're to navigate the changing terrain of culture, we must look at our world through the lens of what God's unchanging words say. They guide us and serve as a solid foundation through any cultural movement. When we follow Him, we don't allow culture to change our standards and views on issues and topics. We remain steady, guided into the same truth that we were shown by our spiritual ancestors. And one day, we'll want to take our kids to explore that truth themselves. It will be there, familiar and unchanged, ready for them to discover, just like it was for us.

Can I Have My Own Truth?

Have you ever noticed how kids have some wild perceptions of reality floating around in that still-developing brain of theirs? Mine (Mark) sure do.

One of my kids was convinced alligators could fly.

One thought that Medieval Times was the castle from Disney World.

One labeled every color as blue.

One insisted he was old enough to drive—at the age of five.

Part of a parent's job is to teach their kids what's true. *The stove is hot. The street is dangerous. The Chicago Bulls are our sports team.* You know, all the essentials.

But then, kids get older—and the world says truth is up to *us* to choose, rather than a reality to be taught.

Our culture's approach to truth can be summarized in phrases like "live your truth" or "own your truth." According to these messages, what's true for you, might be different for me. We get to choose, based on our experience, what makes us feel good or what we're comfortable with. The way culture frames it, truth centers entirely on us. When it comes to favorite foods, favorite movies, or anything else opinion or preference-based—that may be fine. The problem is our culture has taken this thinking—that people can determine their own personal truth—into the spiritual realm. Culture wants us to believe that *we* can determine what is right and wrong, even when that conflicts with what the Bible says.

Jesus had a very different take, and His words hold more weight than anyone's opinion. He said, "I am the way, and the truth, and the life. No one comes to the Father except through me" (John 14:6).

He establishes Himself as truth. He eliminates the idea that we can make our own truth. There is no other truth—and Jesus doesn't put that up for debate. Jesus says no one finds another way except through Him.

I know, how exclusive, right? Well, at least that's what our culture would say. Our world tries to eliminate that uncomfortable feeling of exclusivity. Culture insists there's a buffet of truth to feast on, depending on our own personal tastes. *Everyone can be happy and comfortable with their decisions* . . . mainly because they're based entirely on their personal feelings, opinions, and preferences.

But is everyone actually happier when they choose their own truth? Not in the long run.

"For the wrath of God is revealed from heaven against all ungodliness and unrighteousness of men, who by their unrighteousness suppress the truth" (Romans 1:18).

Verse 25 says that they "exchanged the truth about God for a lie." Even in Bible times, people tried the very thing our culture preaches now—to trade out what God says is true for what they decide they *want* to be truth. They were like kids, insisting on their own way.

How did that tactic work out for them? It was met with the fair judgment of God. When we revolve truth around us instead of the truth of Jesus, we're setting ourselves up to reap the consequences that come from sinning against God.

The truth is ancient, not new. "Thus says the Lord: 'Stand by the roads, and look, and ask for the ancient paths, where the good way is; and walk in it, and find rest for your souls. But they said, 'We will not walk in it'" (Jeremiah 6:16). People have been rejecting God's truth since the beginning of time . . . and they miss so much. **–Tim**

The Israelites learned this the hard way in the book of Judges. Over and over, we see them do what they saw to be right in their own eyes. They rebelled against the words of God and lived their own truth according to their own standards. They always ended up devastated with the consequences of their choices and begged God to rescue them.

Our goal then, is to embrace truth according to what *God* says. We let His Word teach us what's true, like a parent teaches their child. We bring our experience and preferences under submission to His standards. And as we do, we'll function less like a child in the world, and more like a mature man of God.

46

God Is Merciful and Loving . . . So Why Wouldn't There Be More Than One Way into Heaven?

Have you ever noticed how many different books and plans exist for weight loss? Everybody's an expert. The "truth" all these so-called experts share about diet and exercise varies and conflicts to insane degrees. If I (Tim) really wanted to lose weight—and keep it off—I'd get completely frustrated, thinking: *Would somebody just tell me the right way?*

Now let's think about the infinitely more important topic of eternal life in heaven. In a world of so many different religions, books, and voices with conflicting messages, we could end up entirely frustrated as well. *Would somebody please just tell me the right way?*

And that's exactly what God did. The Bible says there is one way to heaven. One. God didn't allow for ten ways. If He did, we could never be sure we were on the right path. It's a merciful thing on God's part to provide only one way; and with it the assurance that we're on the right road.

"I write these things to you who believe in the name of the Son of God, that you may know that you have eternal life" (1 John 5:13).

Man tends to make their own religions—and rules. But God, in His great mercy, didn't leave us at the mercy of all that confusion. He makes it clear in the Bible that there's only one way to heaven. We don't have to fear death, because He says we can know that we have eternal life.

Mercy is when someone has compassion and relents from exercising their justifiable wrath. We deserve eternal separation and punishment from God because of our sin. The fact that there's even *one* way to be forgiven is by definition, merciful. Adding more ways to receive that compassion wouldn't actually make God any more merciful. **—Mark**

As a Man Who Strives to Love Others, Do I Need to Accept Everyone Else's Beliefs as Being Okay?

Let's look at Jesus' example. Did He love others? Absolutely. Did He treat everyone else's beliefs as if He approved of their views? Absolutely not.

Sometimes I (Tim) hear people say that Jesus accepted people where they were—and that we should too. That suggests that we also need to accept their beliefs—which is not right at all. The thing is, Jesus didn't *accept* people where they were. He *met* people where they were. He didn't wait for them to show up at His door—or the synagogue. He went to where they were. He showed them love. Shared the truth. And if they were willing to follow? He led them on a new path. Jesus met people *where* they were so He could *change* them into the person He'd made them to be. That's massively different from accepting people where they are.

■ ■ ■

Mark: In love, God sent Jesus, wanting people to believe in Him. That's what John 3:16 tells us. For many, that meant changing their beliefs and altering their life entirely. Jesus didn't come to earth saying, "Do your thing, live your truth, just be you!" His message called people to repent . . . to change directions and follow Him, but it was still entirely loving. When we point others to believe in Jesus, we can do it in love, just like our God did for us.

■ ■ ■

The problem is, we've forgotten to love those we disagree with. Christians who disagree with the beliefs of others in the church, their family, or in our culture are often expressing their differences in mean-spirited, unbiblical, and unloving ways. It's gotten ugly. That wasn't Jesus' way at all. Look at how Jesus showed love to people who didn't share His views, convictions, or lifestyle.

> ***Nicodemus, the Pharisee*** (John 3). Religious leaders had so massively misinterpreted God's truth, but Jesus met Nicodemus where he was. Jesus shared truth—and how Nicodemus could be saved.
>
> ***The woman caught in adultery*** (John 8). She'd totally twisted God's plan for sex. Jesus protected her from a mob bent on killing her. He met her where she was and offered her forgiveness and a new life path to follow.
>
> ***The demon-possessed man of the tombs*** (Mark 5). This guy was a wild man—and under the control of Jesus' enemy. While others would naturally steer clear of the man, Jesus met him where he was and freed him from slavery to Satan. He gave him a new life and purpose.

If Christians are to love others, let's not do some of the unloving things Christians often do. *Here are some examples.*

- Unfriending those who don't share our viewpoints.
- Getting into heated debates, or rude, belittling, prideful,

sarcastic social media exchanges over cultural, political, and social issues.

- Letting our viewpoints become a "me vs. them" divider in the family, church, school, workplace, or with neighbors.

So, how do I love those with views who differ from mine? We'll tackle that in the next question.

48
Can I Disagree with Someone and Still Love Them?

Our culture has lifted up "tolerance" as the crown jewel of what loving others should look like; as though giving our approval is the highest form of love, even when we disagree with the views or choices of others. In my (Tim) opinion, this creates two dilemmas.

> ***We fail as protectors.*** We can get gun-shy about speaking up and expressing biblical viewpoints that differ from those of the people we're with. Christians are supposed to be loving, right? We may think, *If I open my mouth, I'll be labeled as a bigot, as being close-minded, or as being a "hater," and I'll do harm to the cause of Christ.* But as men, we're to protect others. Being "tolerant" isn't the best way to do that.
>
> ***Others miss the chance to hear the truth.*** Culture basically says it's unloving to disagree with others. But if Jesus hadn't cared enough to share the truth with

Nicodemus, he wouldn't have known how to truly be saved. If Jesus hadn't cared enough to interact with the man of the tombs in Mark 5, he would've never been freed.

So, how do I love someone I disagree with?

Pray for them. Ask God to help you keep the bigger picture (eternity) in mind.

Ask God to help you watch what you say or write. If you find yourself itching to throw your opinion in, that might be the wrong time to speak up. And when we're with certain people, we're best off avoiding certain subjects.

Look for opportunities to share truth—in love. "Whoever gives an honest answer kisses the lips" (Proverbs 24:26). An interesting verse, right? In Bible times, a kiss on the cheek was an accepted way of greeting others, like a handshake. But a kiss on the *lips* was a sign of love. This verse says being honest and sharing truth in a kind, loving way is a sign of love—not hate. Our enemy has used our culture to redefine love and hate. Our culture wrongly teaches that loving someone means we shouldn't disagree with them—even if their viewpoint goes against what God says in His Word.

Watch our tone. The way we share and say things makes all the difference.

Stop "canceling" those you disagree with. Cutting off friendships, family members, or family functions cuts off your ability to show them Christ's love.

Look at the person beyond the issues you differ on. Imagine if someone attacked them—and you were there. You'd jump in to help defend them, right? Keep that mindset. Why not be there for them now?

Actions speak louder than words. Look for ways to demonstrate love. Helping them. Encouraging them. By being kind to them consistently and creatively, we often gain their respect. It's awfully hard for someone to attack a person they respect, right? When we've been intentional about showing love and kindness, that often opens doors for us to kindly speak into their lives with truth too. Let's be good examples of a follower of Christ in everything we do. "Let no one despise you for your youth, but set the believers an example in speech, in conduct, in love, in faith, in purity" (1 Timothy 4:12).

There'll always be people in our life with viewpoints we don't agree with. But that shouldn't reduce the love we show them.

When we continue to love people—even those we disagree with—it demonstrates a strength in our manhood that's magnetic and rare. It's this kind of love that makes the world stand up and notice. That's how Jesus loved.

49
How Can a Man Love Someone He Can't Fully Respect?

Love and respect are different. I (Tim) may have really good reasons not to respect someone. But I can still *love* them—and as a Christian, I need to. Let's think of love not so much as some emotion or feeling, but more as an action verb.

In the Bible, 1 Corinthians 13 describes elements of love that we're to demonstrate toward others. Even though I don't fully *respect* someone, with God's help I can . . .

> Be kind and patient and not be rude or easily irritated by them.
>
> Be dependable, not letting them down.
>
> Be more flexible, not insisting on my way.
>
> Be more forgiving.

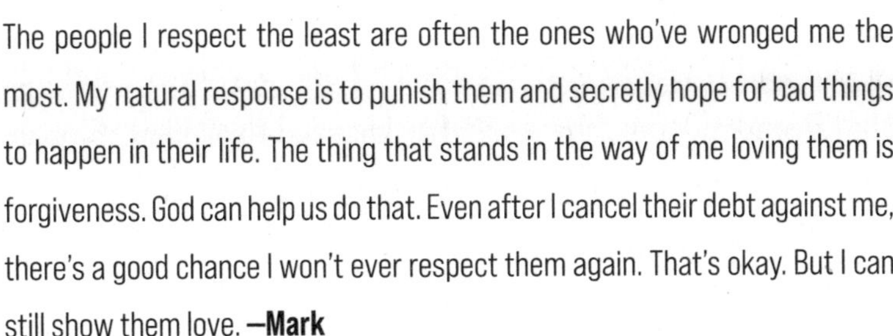

The people I respect the least are often the ones who've wronged me the most. My natural response is to punish them and secretly hope for bad things to happen in their life. The thing that stands in the way of me loving them is forgiveness. God can help us do that. Even after I cancel their debt against me, there's a good chance I won't ever respect them again. That's okay. But I can still show them love. **—Mark**

We aren't going to succeed at loving someone we don't respect unless we're putting the Foundational Five into practice. We definitely need self-control and Holy Spirit control for this one!

Sometimes it also helps me if I try to see that person as I imagine Jesus sees them. Praying for them helps me do that. Or I picture them when they were younger—before they developed the attitudes, behavior, or viewpoints I don't respect.

Men who show love to others—even people they can't respect—stand out in good ways. That's living out God's design for the man He wants us to become.

50

Is There More Than Just Male or Female? Is It Possible for Our Masculine Identity to Be Fluid—or to Change?

Just in my (Mark) lifetime alone, the way culture approaches this topic has shifted dramatically. From the way we talk about it, to the way we've legislated it, to the ways society celebrates it . . . things look very different now than they did even a decade ago. Which makes this topic one of the more important ones to talk through.

Our goal is to let God's Word define the way we see and talk about gender. While the world has changed their view on male and female, God hasn't. His word is clear and consistent. Let's start in the beginning.

Genesis 1:27 says, "So God created man in his own image, in the image of God he created him; male and female he created them." There's actually a ton in this one verse alone. Let's break it down:

God created: Humanity was created by God. Since He's holy and perfect, it's impossible for Him to make a mistake. We see that later in verse 31. God looks out over His creation and calls it all "very good." There was nothing to improve upon. Everything was exactly as it should be. To try and change ourselves from how we were created or identify as anything other than how we are created, would imply that God made a mistake.

In His image: This means humans have a likeness to God that no other creation does. There's something within our maleness that represents God. No person of the Trinity has altered their identity. The Father has always been the Father. Same with the Son and Spirit. If the Trinity's identity is not fluid, neither should ours be.

Male and female He created them: God established male and female from the beginning. If God created them, He gets to define their function and purpose. To reject your physical sex you were born with is to reject the God-given purpose He gave you at birth.

Okay, let's move forward one verse. There's something so important here. Genesis 1:28 says, "And God said to them, 'Be fruitful and multiply and fill the earth and subdue it.'" God gave the male and female responsibility here on earth. One of those jobs? Multiply. In other words, have kids. Which means . . . have sex. Fulfilling that command relies specifically on a male being the male as he was physically created, and a female being a female as she was created to be.

Here's my point. God created their bodies in ways that enabled them to carry out the responsibility He gave them. They fit together, quite literally. If Adam rejected his maleness, it would have simultaneously worked against his God-given responsibility.

Anytime we go against the purpose and instruction of God, it's sin. If it would have been sin for Adam, then it's also sin for us.

I'm not saying it's a sin if we don't have kids. I *am* saying that rejecting our physical sex is also a rejection of our God-given design, purpose, and earthly responsibility. And rejecting or rebelling against God's purpose for us definitely *is* sin.

The creation account establishes the way God designed male and female to function in the world. We see the purpose begin in Genesis and run through the rest of Scripture. That consistent teaching gives us all we need to view this topic with the right perspective . . . the way God does.

51

What Does the Christian Life Look Like for Someone with Same-Sex Attraction?

To answer this question, we first need a brief theology of sex. The way I (Mark) read the Bible, sex was created by God for a few reasons.

> ***It's the method God gave humans to carry out His command in Genesis 1:28 to multiply and fill the earth*** (yes, that's where babies come from).
>
> ***It's also part of how God brings a man and woman (Adam and Eve) together as one flesh in Genesis 1:24.*** Which means God designed sex to belong solely between a man and woman, in the covenant of marriage.

> ***God designed sex to be enjoyable.*** He wants it to be a pleasurable experience between a husband and wife (reference Song of Solomon if you have any doubts here).
>
> ***God gave us sex to keep us united to our spouse.*** First Corinthians 7:5–6 tells us to avoid abstaining from sexual relations for an extended time because it allows Satan to tempt us. The intimacy and pleasure of sex helps keep the bond between a husband and wife strong.

These are God's purposes for sex. Pretty great, right? In God's eyes, sex is good and part of how He blesses us. Within church circles a lot of what we hear about is the danger of sex—and to avoid it. At its foundation, sex is good and should be celebrated. That is, as long as we do it God's way.

The temptation with sex is to change the God-given purposes and start to enjoy it in ways God never intended. Any time we desire or practice sex different from how God created it to be, we sin. Lust, adultery, sex outside of marriage, sexual relations/marriage with the same sex—our culture has all sorts of ways to pursue sex differently from what God created it for.

This is where our culture says things like "love is love," as if the feeling of love makes breaking God's laws okay. But following our heart instead of God's plan never works out well. Whether we're attracted to men or women, our heart finds ways to make sex about us and what we want, instead of what is best for us according to God's plan.

Our goal then, is to align our sexual desires and practices with God's good purposes. This will require us train our hearts to pursue sex in the way He designed it to be enjoyed. For many men, this means disciplining his mind not to lust after women—and exercising the self-control not to have sex with a woman before marriage. For a married man, following God's purposes for sex means staying faithful to his wife and enjoying the gift of sex within that covenant relationship.

For those who struggle with same-sex attraction, the goal is still to align their practices with God's purposes.

- That means abstaining from any intimate or physical relationship with another guy, since that's reserved for men and women joined in marriage.
- It will also require him to avoid lusting for another man, since lust also strays from God's plan.

He might struggle with attraction to men for the rest of his life, but he is not free to pursue or entertain those thoughts, because they never lead to God's purpose for sex.

Our enemy, the devil, wants to mess up God's plan for sex by causing us to want something outside the boundaries. Heterosexual men and same-sex-attracted men both have a temptation battle. Both will need to put to death their sexual desires that fall outside the covenant of marriage between a man and a woman. While culture promotes indulging in every kind of sexual pleasure someone pleases, the follower of Jesus strives for the narrow way.

■ ■ ■

Tim: For heterosexual or same-sex-attracted men . . . there is hope in the battle to honor God's plan for sex. Both self-control and Holy Spirit–control are critically important in that fight. We talked about them in the Foundational Five. And asking God to change your desires *works*. He made our hearts . . . and can change them if we're brave enough to ask Him to.

One more thought on this. For some, maybe those desires don't disappear—or maybe not for a long time. Don't think that God isn't hearing you—or that He doesn't care. Ask God to make your desire to be faithful to Him *so* strong, that you'll resist the temptations to pursue a same-sex attraction. The testimony I've heard from other men is that God has honored that prayer.

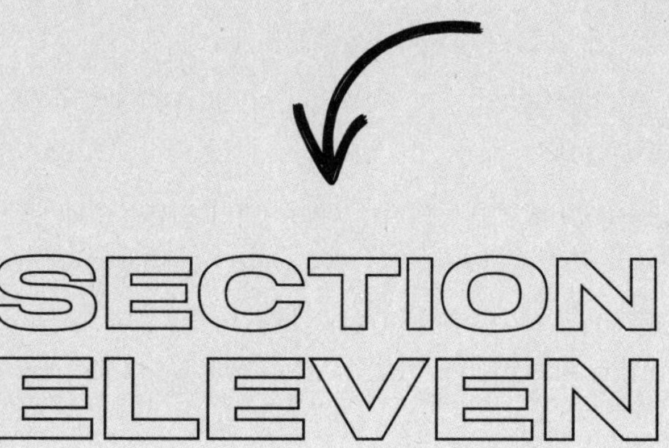

SECTION ELEVEN

WORK

I (Tim) knew an employer looking to hire a maintenance supervisor. For each applicant, he conducted a short interview followed by a walking tour of the facilities. Just before the tour, he slipped out to the plant, balled up a piece of paper, and tossed it onto the floor.

Applicant after applicant walked the building with him—seemingly fascinated by everything. Maybe they never saw the scrap on the floor—or thought it would be rude to divert their attention from the boss for the two seconds it'd take to pick it up. But every person failed the test. Except one. While getting the tour, one man nonchalantly picked up the ball of paper and tossed it in a garbage can as they passed.

The boss hired him on the spot.

The employer wasn't interested in polished résumés or guys who interviewed well. He wanted someone who'd show initiative and keep the facilities looking terrific.

Our work habits say plenty about us as men. And if we're followers of Christ, how we do our work is a direct reflection on Him.

What Does My Work Have to Do with Being a Man?

I (Mark) never liked the polling job. I don't know what I dreaded more, the 4:00 a.m. wakeup call or the seventeen-hour workday. There were lines of impatient, complaining voters. And there were machines that malfunctioned and needed my "expert" tech support. Why did I sign up year after year to work at the polling place on election day? Because for a college student, the couple hundred bucks they paid was good money. I justified the work drudgery for the resulting paycheck.

Our world tends to approach work like that. It's a means to an end. We work so we can fund the lifestyle we want. Our work becomes less about what we do, and more about what we get from it. There's a lot we can gain from a job. Social status, authority, experiences, personal satisfaction, or maybe we just do it all for the store discount.

Not all of that is wrong. But, if we reduce our work down to a transaction like I did with working the polling place, we'll miss the role work is supposed to play in our life as men.

The Bible gives us a much richer perspective of work. It goes back to Adam in the garden. Check out Genesis 2:15. "The LORD God took the man and put him in the garden of Eden to work it and keep it."

Adam had a job! God not only gave him tasks, He created the very idea of work. Part of the purpose of work links back to Genesis 1:28. God told Adam to "subdue" the earth, which means to bring under control. This is what Adam was doing in the garden. As he cultivated it, he brought it under control. What was once wild became organized and productive. His work benefitted the garden and all who enjoyed the food it produced.

As workers, we bring God's same work "mandate" into the world. We're to establish order and beauty out of things that otherwise would lack it. We create, manage, and build in a way that represents God to the world. We take ideas and form them into a vision and a plan. We gather people and make them a team. We take random ingredients and turn them into the most amazing latte. When we do that . . . we work. And when we work, we do one of the most foundational things God made us to do.

There's one more detail from this verse I don't want us to miss. Notice, Adam worked in the garden *before* they ate the fruit and sinned. Which means, *work is not a result of sin*. Work was created as an integral element of life in paradise. It was designed as part of the purest good of Eden—*before* sin changed everything. God's plans for our lives include work. Doing our work well is part of what it means to live a full and satisfied life. I even think work will be part of our eternal paradise in heaven.

We often view work as something we're stuck with—or as some kind of punishment. But from the beginning, it was part of a perfect life God had created. Work isn't a shift to wait out, or just about a check to collect. Work is a necessary good in our life and will be part of how we worship God in eternity.

Are you seeing the disconnect between God's purpose for work and what we've turned it into? Work isn't something we use to get things we want out of life. It's a gift of life we get to live out. When we work with His purpose, our days bring God glory, just as Adam did in the garden. Whether we're on shift as a paramedic or wrapping up a recording session at the studio . . . it's good . . . it's worship . . . it's work!

Can you imagine how our job might change if we remembered work is a gift from God? We'll do less complaining and more encouraging. We'll work harder and take more pride in the job we do. We'll look to make work easier for others instead of having the "that's not my job" mentality. Having that attitude will make our job less boring, more fun, and will likely make the boss wish he had more workers just like us! **–Tim**

What Work Habits Set a Man Up for Success?

You and I (Tim) need the right perspective if we're going to do well at work.

> ***Know who the real boss is.*** As Christians, we work for the Lord. Our earthly boss may be a jerk—and we'll be tempted not to give work our full effort. But our God is good, and ultimately, we work for Him. He's worthy of our best efforts, right?
>
> ***Work as if the boss is always watching—because He is.*** Our employer may not always be looking over our shoulder, but God doesn't miss anything. Doing our best—even when a supervisor isn't present—is all about honesty, integrity, and honor.
>
> ***Beware of the "I deserve more" syndrome.*** It's easy to start thinking that we're worth more or that we are underappreciated. That attitude leads to complaining and poor work habits. When we sense this happening, remember that we work for the Lord, and trust Him for the pay we need.

Ten good work habits to build:

1. *Dependable.* If you say you're going to be there, be there on time—and ready to work.
2. *Responsible.* Get your work done right, on time, and without needing reminders.

3. *Trustworthy and honest.* You may have access to the building, money, tools, machinery, or inventory. Treat them like they belong to God.

4. *Initiative.* Notice things that need doing and get them done before you're asked.

5. *Set the pace.* We've been hired to work to the best of our ability—and to make our supervisor's job easier. Others may slack off, but let's make sure *we're* hustling.

6. *Set the tone.* As Christians, we're to have joy. If we don't, we need to address that. Bring that joy to work and give the place a better work atmosphere for everyone.

7. *Show we care.* Every coworker and supervisor have hardships. Let's be an encourager. Show Christ's love.

8. *Follow up.* Whatever work we finish, give it one last quality check. If appropriate, touch base with customers to be sure they're satisfied. It's amazing the difference it makes.

9. *Take the blame and share the credit.* When something goes wrong, shoulder the responsibility rather than pointing the finger. When we get a pat on the back, let's include the others who contributed to our success.

10. *Stay balanced.* Many men treat work like it's the most important thing in life. We must be careful not to make work our god—or what defines us. If work causes us to neglect family, church, or to rush through our time with God? We're off balance. People who lose their balance fall.

One way I've stayed balanced over the years has been with a routine of Sabbath. A Sabbath day takes a full stop from work to rest, enjoy, and worship. **—Mark**

As we pay attention and put into practice the Foundational Five, all of the above become easier and more doable. Let's never forget that the ability to work is a huge gift.

54

What's the Difference Between "Downtime" and Wasting Time?

I'm (Tim) not always working—and you won't be either. What do we do with our free time? To answer that question, let's remember that *time* is a gift from God. He gives us so much time—and then our life on earth is through.

Wasting time is largely about doing things that have no—or have negative—eternal benefits. Sometimes phone-scrolling is wasting time. Same with excessive gaming or binge-watching a series. Wasting time is often about stalling off something we know we need to do.

Downtime may have some of the same activities, but the outcome is different. Downtime is about recharging our batteries. Downtime is something we need to strategically build into our day. After we've done something to relax, we should be fresher, more balanced, and better prepared for whatever God has for us to do next.

▪ ▪ ▪

Mark: People are usually on either end of extremes with this. They either never take downtime, or they take far too many breaks. No matter which way you lean, I think both are helped by doing this one thing every week. Take time (for me it's Sunday night . . . most of the time 15–30 minutes) to schedule out your week and set priorities, the things that are most important and need to get done. My dad makes a physical checklist for every single day. I have it all in my phone. It helps us stay focused to do our work well and also know when we need to stop. I lean too far in the direction of work, so when I make my schedule, I make sure that I see open space. I'll even schedule in hobbies or other things I enjoy. A weekly list helps me stay disciplined and intentional on the right things and keeps me balanced so I don't over—or under work.

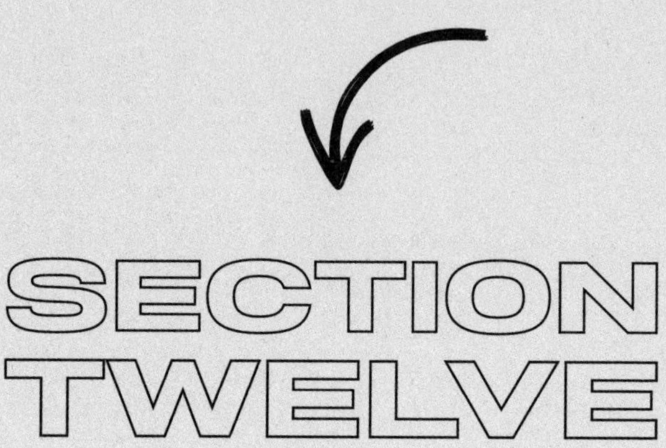

SECTION TWELVE

PORNOGRAPHY

I (Tim) had just finished speaking at a men's conference. The topic? The lethal impact of pornography on men—and how to break free. Afterward, a young man with haunted eyes approached me and held out his phone.

"Take it." There was no hiding the desperation in his voice. "*Take it.* I don't want it anymore."

His phone was his portal to access porn. But he was seeing that the portal works both ways. Porn had reached back and grabbed *him*. And that cadaverous hand of porn wasn't letting go. It wasn't just guilt or remorse that I saw in his eyes. It was terror.

We've talked about the Foundational Five . . . those essential areas we must focus on to become the man God designed us to be. Pornography has the power to derail all five of them.

> ***Your sense of purpose.*** God has things He's planned for you to do. Porn will stop a man from doing them—and keep him from becoming the man God wants him to become. Viewing porn is disobeying God . . . and a man will never attain God's best plans for him when he refuses to repent and truly change direction.
>
> ***Self-control.*** Viewing porn undoes self-control. Porn is about self-satisfying. A selfish man hurts himself and others in so many ways.
>
> ***Holy Spirit–control.*** The Bible is clear that porn is wrong. And if we choose sin anyway, we quench the Spirit, and He won't be doing His powerful work in our life. We're rejecting the provider of wisdom . . . and our source of supernatural love, joy, peace, patience, kindness, self-control, and more.
>
> ***Abiding in Christ.*** When viewing porn, men choose the company of sin and darkness. That isn't how we abide. Choosing porn is turning your back on Jesus—the one who died to rescue us from sin's grip and the penalty of sin.

> ***Putting the Word into practice.*** We know the Bible is our guide, but choosing porn is the opposite of putting the Bible into practice. We're leaving ourselves vulnerable and unprotected. We're foolishly setting ourselves up for massive loss.

The fact that porn is so effective in derailing the Foundational Five makes it powerfully dangerous. Oh, yeah . . . porn will undo every aspect of you becoming the good, effective Christian man God designed you to be.

Is *That* Pornography?

My wife still teases me about it, which I'll admit, I (Mark) deserve. It was a few years back, and I needed to renew my driver's license. I'd put it off for months because, really . . . who likes going to the DMV? And then one morning, I received a text from the Secretary of State saying I could renew my license through an online form. Wow, so helpful! They even included a link to the form within the text.

I filled it out as I got ready for work. It wasn't a long form. They just needed the basics—like my date of birth, driver's license number, address, and my Social Security number. So easy!

You should've seen my wife's face when I excitedly told her that we could check that off our to-do list. She clearly identified what I'd failed to see. I'd been scammed!

I'd missed the danger behind the text, all because I'd identified it incorrectly. I labeled it as helpful and harmless—instead of a dangerous scam designed to steal my identity. I've seen guys do something similar with porn. They consume various forms of pornography but never think about it as *actually porn*. They normalize something dangerous, and label it as harmless.

The best way to label it correctly is to start with a description, as definitions vary and can even be too narrow. Porn is designed to stimulate erotic feelings. Such stimulation can come from things like pictures of women in lingerie or a texted photo of a body part, images we may not define per se as porn, but that have an erotic effect.

We typically only identify the most extreme examples as porn, like nude images of people we've never met—or a video of people doing sexual acts together. But going back to the description above, there's more that needs to be categorized within the label of porn. Things like:

Nudity through text or on Snapchat

Some anime

Sex scenes or partial nudity in shows/movies

Some online chat forums

Some Instagram profiles and reels

Some comics, graphic novels, romance novels

Some music lyrics

All of this should be considered porn—and that list could be a lot longer! But people immerse themselves in this stuff every day and never think they have a porn problem or that they're in danger. That's like falling for a different scam text every day.

If it's arousing to you, consider it porn. I knew a man who avoided a certain wing of the mall—just so he wouldn't walk by the big-name lingerie store. The lingerie worn by the mannequins and by models on display pictures were pornographic to him. **—Tim**

Speaking of the scam text, what happened with that? Nothing. I never got hacked. My identity wasn't stolen. Not because the scam was harmless, but because I saw the danger and did something about it. I immediately bought identity protection. I put up safeguards and avoided the very thing that had caught me off guard. As men, we'd be wise to do the same with the porn that surrounds us. Identify it for what it truly is, put up safeguards that protect us, and put distance between us and the danger. Let's talk more about that in the sections ahead.

56
Is Porn Okay—As Long as It Doesn't Turn into an Addiction?

No. I'm (Tim) telling you: Porn is *not* okay. That's like asking if murder is okay as long as we don't make a habit of it. Porn is a deadly sin that will hurt us and others—guaranteed—because that's what God's Word teaches.

Check out these verses that urge us to steer clear of women who have sex outside of marriage for pay or some other reason. That is exactly the type of women involved in pornography. They will destroy you.

"And now, O sons, listen to me, and be attentive to the words of my mouth. Let not your heart turn aside to her ways; do not stray into her paths, for many a victim has she laid low, and all her slain are a mighty throng. Her house is the way to Sheol, going down to the chambers of death" (Proverbs 7:24–27).

Her house leads to the chambers of death.

Death of dreams.

Death of God's plan for our life.

Death of self-respect.

Death of respect from those who love us.

Death of relationships with those we love.

Scary, scary thoughts, right? And as porn takes men down, it destroys others in the process.

Those who look up to them.

Those who depend on them.

Those who love them.

The very ones they want to protect.

"But I'm not addicted." So many young men say this—and they may even believe it. The truth? Men are addicted long before they realize it. So, here's a question. Say a man views porn—realizes it's wrong and that it'll hurt himself and others—but instead of quitting, he goes back to it again? What else is that other than an addiction?

Others say that a Christian can't be addicted to porn because they've been set free from sin. Yes, I get it, but Romans 6 warns us not to let sin reign in our bodies. We can choose to become slaves to sin. To let sin have mastery over us. When we choose to disobey God's Word, we allow sin to get a fresh grip in our life again. It gets easier and easier to choose sin, and harder and harder to break free.

"I can go days—weeks without viewing porn. That proves I'm not addicted." But in between viewing porn, how often does that man *think* about porn? Does he look forward to the next time he can view it—even though he knows it's wrong? That sounds like addiction.

And if a Christian man believes he *is* addicted to porn, that doesn't give him a pass to keep sinning. "I can't help myself. I'm addicted." That's no excuse. Jesus sets prisoners free—and that man is choosing not to follow Christ with his whole heart.

Whether you term it an addiction or not, you must break free. And you can, with God's help.

■ ■ ■

Mark: I know an elder of a church who asks every new staff hire the same question, "When was the last time you viewed porn?" He doesn't ask if you have a porn problem or addiction, because he knows people have the tendency to define addiction differently. The truth is, that elder knows that even occasional viewing of porn will be a massive problem in the life of any potential hire. If you justify porn consumption as "only a little," or "not addicted," or "not a problem," you likely don't understand how dangerous this sin truly is.

Isn't It Better to Look at Porn Than to Have Sex Before Marriage?

That's like asking me (Tim) if it's okay to commit one type of sin to keep me from committing another type.

"I'm only swiping a little money from my dad's wallet. It's not like I'm robbing a bank." Sorry. Either way it's still stealing. It's still sin. As Christian men, we're to avoid sin, period.

Now, some might argue that having sex with someone before marriage potentially leads to a whole lot more complications than hiding in some dark corner, viewing porn by themselves. On the surface, that almost seems logical. But it's a flawed argument. Viewing porn is sin—just with different consequences than having sex with someone outside of marriage.

One of those complications? Viewing porn actually makes a man increasingly less prepared for marriage. It guts the Foundational Five (things he'll need to be a good husband) in their life like we mentioned in the opener for this section. And men viewing porn abandon their role as protector. Men viewing porn support an industry that uses, abuses, and enslaves women and girls.

A young man who sees porn as a good compromise, rationalizing that using porn is a way to survive until marriage without having sex, is falling for the devil's lie. He'll never be ready for marriage as long as he's into porn. It's a vicious cycle.

A man who uses porn to help "make it" until their wedding day will have massive problems in marriage.

- He's developed horrible habits of self-indulgence and instant gratification. If a man's bride doesn't want sex as often as he's built the habit of viewing porn and satisfying himself—he'll have tremendous conflict.

- Porn twists a man's tastes. Porn is built on lust—not love. That's what this man will bring into his marriage. Selfish sexual appetites. That'll lead to massive hurt and problems.

- A man who's into porn before marriage will likely go back to it even after he's married. He never developed the needed self-control to say no to porn. His wife will find out . . . and she'll see that as him being unfaithful. She'll lose respect for him. That leads to excruciating pain for both of them—and a lot less sex.

I can't tell you the number of men I've talked to who severely damaged or ruined a marriage because they hadn't broken free from porn before marrying.

58

I Keep Going Back to Porn. How Do I Stop?

I've (Tim) seen countless men struggle with this. Those who succeed in breaking free? It always comes down to putting the Foundational Five into practice—and often a couple of other things we'll look at here.

Your sense of purpose. God has some things He's planned for you to do. Remember that. Reread Ephesians 2:10.

Our enemy doesn't want you to experience the massive fulfillment you'll find in becoming the man God has designed you to be. ***You can't have porn—and live out God's purpose for your life.*** Believe that. Are you ready to fight for the good things God has planned for you? Good . . . you'll need that.

Self-control. When speaking to a crowd of listeners about fighting sexual sin, Jesus said this to describe how ruthless men need to be.

"You have heard that it was said, 'You shall not commit adultery.' But I say to you that everyone who looks at a woman with lustful intent has already committed adultery with her in his heart. If your right eye causes you to sin, tear it out and throw it away. For it is better that you lose one of your members than that your whole body be thrown into hell. And if your right hand causes you to sin, cut it off and throw it away. For it is better that you lose one of your members than that your whole body go into hell'" (Matthew 5:27–30).

This is about cutting the things out of your life that cause you to go back to porn. You have to be brutal. That was what the young man at that conference was doing when he handed me his phone. He was gouging away the things that caused him to sin.

Holy Spirit–control. The Holy Spirit . . . the power of God in us. You need a heart change if you're going to break free from pornography. A change of desires. You have to *want* to break free. The more you surrender to God—and give permission for the Holy Spirit to change your heart . . . your desires . . . the more you'll find victory over porn. Self-control is a fruit of the Holy Spirit. So, the more you surrender to the Holy Spirit and ask Him to control you, the more self-control He pours into your life.

I've known guys who've turned in their smartphone for a flip phone. Guys who've destroyed their iPad or laptop. Men who've taken the internet completely out of their house. All of this . . . to battle the sin that so easily entangled them. Sounds extreme? They'd say it was necessary. And worth it. **—Mark**

Abiding in Christ. You aren't going to beat porn without the help of Jesus. The Bible says *He* sets prisoners free . . . so stay close to Him. Stay connected.

Putting the Word into Practice. Without obeying what the Bible says, you have no foundation. No protection when the storms of temptation come. You need to build habits of doing what the Bible says. Memorizing Scripture verses will help a man remember—and have the strength to do what the Bible says in every area of life.

Accountability. Many think this is the big answer to beating porn. It's not. The tools listed above are actually more effective. Accountability has its place and can be a very useful tool—but only if you've put the Foundational Five into play. Here's the secret to making accountability more powerful. Choose to be accountable to someone who has teeth. If your accountability partner is too easy on you every time you mess up, the accountability tool isn't nearly as effective. Who would you absolutely hate to talk to about messing up and viewing porn? A parent? A grandparent? Those are the ones you want for accountability partners.

The most effective form of accountability I've seen is through phone/laptop software. When someone knows that any inappropriate content will be flagged and will immediately notify their accountability partner, it makes them think twice. There's a number of software options. Our church staff uses Covenant Eyes and has found it to be top tier. **—Mark**

Professional help. Sometimes a Christian biblical counselor or psychologist is a good idea when it comes to understanding why you keep going back to porn—so you can more effectively fight it.

I've consistently seen four things when men go to battle to rid porn from their life.

1. *Often the battle is long and hard.* Maybe God doesn't free them instantly so they're less likely to return to porn later. They'll remember how hard it was to beat.

2. *Victory is absolutely possible.* I've heard conference speakers say that all men will struggle with lust until death. Like lust is a life sentence with no hope of parole. That simply isn't true. More likely, that *speaker* hasn't been set free yet. Don't let his experience diminish yours. Psalm 107 tells us that the Lord sets prisoners free. Don't settle for anything less. Will men freed from porn need to stay on guard? Yes, very much like alcoholics, once they've been freed, stay far from alcohol.

3. *The testimony of men who have broken free from porn—with God's help?* They've found life is so much better without porn and they never want to go back to it. They don't secretly wish they could view porn. It's like their eyes have been opened, and they see how deadly porn really is. They're careful not to let it into their life again.

4. *Some give up the fight—and lose some massive things as a result.* Not all who know they need to be free of porn actually break free. Maybe they don't go into the fight with an undivided heart to beat it or something. But the price they pay is devastating.

You *can* break free . . . with God's help. Now is the time.

SECTION THIRTEEN

PARENTS

The way I (Tim) see it, if you were raised by a Christian parent(s), their job pretty much boiled down to a handful of challenging things they had to do for you—besides loving you unconditionally, of course.

Protect. From physical, emotional, and spiritual danger.

Provide. Food. Clothing. Shelter. Education—at least

through high school. Anything beyond that is a bonus, not a requirement.

Prepare. Helping you develop emotionally, physically, mentally, spiritually, and practically to become an effective, responsible adult.

Be present. Modeling what it's like to be a mature Christian and being a good example. And also, just being around, available when you needed them.

Do you have siblings? Then your parents had to do all these things above for you while they were doing the same for your siblings (who probably gave them a lot more headaches than you ever did). Your parents had to do all that while exhausted, scared, distracted, inexperienced, holding down a job—and under attack from the enemy of our souls. An enemy who didn't want them to succeed when it came to raising you. Likely your parents tried to be good parents while simultaneously learning a new job, establishing a career, keeping a marriage strong—or repairing one in trouble.

Your mom or dad probably didn't get all of these things about parenting right. Not all the time. No parent ever did or will. Part of being a man is cutting our parents some major slack. If you turned eighteen last month, on the one hand you could say your dad has been a parent for eighteen years. He had experience. Couldn't he have done better? Then again, he's only been a parent of an eighteen-year-old for a month. That means parents are constantly in uncharted territory. Being a good parent—to kids who are constantly changing—means your parents were always shooting at a moving target. If you have siblings, your mom or dad had to work with different personalities, trying to learn how best to get through to each. Which means each kid is a different moving target. That isn't easy, and even the best parents are going to miss some shots.

All this to say, if you have terrific parents, be grateful. And if your parents seemed to lack in some of these areas, be understanding. You won't be a perfect parent, either. No matter how hard we try, or how much we want to be the best parent in the world, we're going to miss the mark plenty of times. Parenting is harder work than you can imagine right now.

So, if you had a rough go of it as a kid and your parents didn't do well with their parenting job? I'm sorry for you. I truly am. But a man doesn't wallow in self-pity. He doesn't blame his parents for how he turned out. He picks himself up—with God's help—and works on becoming the man God designed him to be.

What Does It Mean to Honor Your Father and Mother as an Adult?

When we grow up, so much changes—or should. Our relationship with our parents is one of those things. The Bible is clear about the need to honor our parents—and the rewards for doing that.

"'Honor your father and mother' (this is the first commandment with a promise), 'that it may go well with you and that you may live long in the land'" (Ephesians 6:2–3).

We honored parents one way when we were younger—and much of that was about obeying them. ***But honoring our parents isn't just something we did as kids.*** The Bible passages talking about honoring parents don't seem to have a time limit. It's a lifelong thing.

Does honoring parents mean we must still obey them even when we're adults? No, that isn't really it. Although if you still live in Mom and Dad's home, you'll have to live by the house rules.

I (Tim) believe honoring parents can take many forms.

> ***How we talk to them . . . our tone.*** Sometimes young men talk down to their parents. They belittle them. But if we muster up a little energy and sound like we're happy to talk to them, happy to hear their voice when they call, we honor them—and probably make their day.
>
> ***How much we talk to them.*** Parents still want to be part of our life. When you treat them as important enough to you to keep them filled in, you honor them. Often you won't feel you have the time to talk. But if you make them feel that talking to them is an inconvenience, you won't be honoring them.
>
> ***How we treat them.*** Do we show them respect? Parents invested the best years of their lives raising us. They made tremendous sacrifices that we're totally unaware of. Their love is stronger than we'll understand until we have our own kids. When we treat them like they're still massively important to us, we honor them.
>
> ***How we show that we value them.*** Seek their help and advice. Listen to them. Be quick to share our good news with them. All these honor parents.

In an effort to establish independence, sometimes guys cut their parents out of their life in unnecessary and unwise ways. For many reading this, there's still a lot of wisdom/help you can receive from your parents. Their advice is a big one. You won't always take it, but even just hearing it will be a benefit to you (and to them). **—Mark**

How we show them grace. Do their views on things seem old-fashioned, unenlightened, sexist, racist, or biased? Showing your concern or disapproval may be entirely appropriate, as long you do that in a loving way. Love covers a ton of sins, right? Love them despite differing viewpoints—and you'll honor them.

How we turn out. This is probably the greatest way we can honor our parents. They invested many years in raising you, while juggling your siblings and jobs and everything else. The kind of man you become will bring your parents honor—or shame. Let's be the type of son who does his parents proud. Your good character, work ethic, dedication to Christ, the way you love and treat others . . . and more brings honor to your parents. And, of course, it's a pretty good thing for us as well!

How Can I Honor a Parent I Don't Even Respect?

This can be tricky. We want to be truthful and not a fake. If Mom or Dad was a bad parent, how can I (Tim) pretend they weren't?

The secret to honoring a parent who wasn't the greatest, is to honor our God—who *is* the greatest. God told us to honor our parents—and He didn't instruct us only to honor the good ones. Honoring our parents is an act of obedience to God. Ultimately, when we honor our parents, we're showing our love to God by obeying Him.

In the previous section, we've already talked about ways to honor parents. In addition, here's some ways to honor parents we don't fully respect.

> ***Forgive them.*** You'll need to work this out with God.
>
> ***Break the failure pattern.*** If your dad was a workaholic, don't repeat history. Dads are honored when sons overcome bad examples and obstacles.
>
> ***Keep them in the loop.*** Resist the urge to cut them from your life. Update them with what's going on with you. Send pictures. Share your good news with them.
>
> ***Come to them for help.*** I say this carefully. When appropriate, rather than pulling up Google when you need to learn how to fix or do something, call Dad.
>
> ***Ask their opinion.*** If they aren't following God, we need to be cautious about this. But we can ask for

their opinion or advice and learn from their experience in areas of their expertise (buying a car, starting a budget, finding an apartment, and so on).

Remember, the greatest way to honor our parents, even those we can't respect, is to become the man God designed us to be. As we grow into becoming a man of character, our parents will be proud of the man we're becoming. That brings them great joy . . . and honor.

61

My Parents Don't Seem to Respect Me and My Choices . . . What Can I Do?

First off, I really hope you aren't the person who thinks you should automatically gain respect from your parents *because* you're over eighteen. I've (Mark) met guys who think that way, and pride is always at the foundation of their thinking. It seems like they feel they're as smart—or smarter than their parents now—and they expect their parents to treat them as equals. Just because we're adults, doesn't mean our parents don't have wisdom to offer.

Second, no matter how badly you want your parents to respect your decisions, it can't be the ultimate goal. If we chase our parents' approval as our highest priority, it's misplaced. Our first priority is to make decisions that line up with God's Word and honor Him. If our parents don't respect choices that line up with God's Word, we always want to pick honoring God over doing the thing that our parents would prefer.

So, if you've got the right balance with the first two above, how do you go about gaining a healthy respect from your mom or dad? I'd start by having a good conversation about it with your parents.

Here's what defines a good conversation:

It aims to understand the other person just as much as you seek to be understood. This will require asking good questions and then . . . actually listening to what they say! By the end of the conversation, you might not agree with their views, but at least you'll understand their perspective.

It honors both sides from start to finish. It matters that you speak respectfully and with love. That means keeping your tone in check and listening without interrupting.

It isn't rushed. Don't try to cram something super important into a quick, passing conversation. I get it, we're busy. But if we're really going to communicate and understand each other, it'll require adequate time.

It's in person. Don't try to do this over text, or even with a phone call. When we sit with each other and talk, it gives us a better chance at connecting and understanding what the other is trying to say. For those who live a long distance away, a video call is a great option.

There's no doubt, a conversation like this takes humility, on both sides! And while there is no guarantee your parents will respect you at the end, you can rest well knowing your heavenly Father does.

■ ■ ■

Tim: How you handle this conversation will build their respect for you—or bulldoze it. Bring paper and a pen. They may give examples of how you're not acting responsibly, making it hard for them to respect you. Take it without arguing or defending yourself. Ask if there's anything else you can do to *earn* their respect. Write everything down so you can work on it. When you handle this conversation with that kind of maturity—their respect for you can't help but go up!

62

How Do I Confront My Parents About Something That Bothers Me?

When you were younger, correcting your parents was probably seen as dishonoring. As you get older, if done right, it can actually be a way we honor them. It all depends on our approach, which is why I (Mark) suggest you ask yourself these questions before getting into the conversation with your parents.

> **Am I the right person to be having this conversation?** It's possible that someone else is better suited to talk through the issue with your parents. Someone like a pastor, one of their good friends, or one of your siblings. If it's something personal between you and them, you should probably take it. But there are

plenty of other scenarios where it's wise to consider who else could initiate the conversation.

Am I confronting sin, or a preference? Thinking through this question will help you develop your approach. Does whatever they're doing that bothers you boil down to the fact that you don't share the same opinion or viewpoint? It's important to recognize that before putting your preferences and expectations on them. If it's sin, you approach it with a different seriousness—knowing you're pointing them to God's standard, not your own personal conviction.

Are my motives in the right place? If you're ready to blast them, you're not ready to have a productive conversation. You want your motive to be love, with a desire to genuinely be helpful.

When is the right time for this conversation? Finding a strategic time to meet with them will be a huge help in this being productive. Find a time when you can focus on this one topic. Choose a place where you won't be distracted and others won't interrupt. In other words, this won't be a text intervention or something you bring up at the family Christmas dinner table.

What words do I want to describe my tone? It's helpful to think about our tone beforehand. As you walk into the conversation, put those words at the

> forefront of your mind. Words like, "Loving. Compassionate. Respectful. Firm. Humble." These help steer your words and actions so that at the end of the conversation, you'll feel good about how you communicated the things on your heart.

As you head into the conversation, keep the Foundational Five in mind. Three of them in particular will be a huge help to you as you prepare for—and then eventually have the talk.

Holy Spirit–control: He'll help you speak in love and give you wisdom for what you should say.

Self-control: I recognize there's a strong possibility this conversation will have high emotions. Self-control keeps you from sinning, no matter how much you might be tempted to.

Let the Bible be your guide: You want your confrontation to be in line with what the Bible says. Not only what you confront them on, but also *how* you choose to confront them.

■ ■ ■

Tim: Mark is absolutely right. You'll honor your parents if you handle the conversation well. That alone says something about the man you're becoming. And remember, this conversation will be hard for your parents. Start out with some reminders of what they're doing right and things you love and appreciate about them *before* bringing up your concerns. Are they your hero? Show that . . . and it will make it easier for them to hear what you have to say.

SECTION FOURTEEN

PRIDE AND HUMILITY

I (Mark) had no idea what I was doing, but there was no way I was going to admit that—or ask anybody questions. Everyone else in the group loved sushi, but this was going to be my first experience. As we looked over the menu, they all talked about what sounded good to them while I listened—and comprehended nothing.

Our appetizer arrived at the table. Something called *edamame*. It looked simple enough. I thought they were some sort of green beans. I wasn't sure if I'd like the sushi, so I intentionally loaded up on these. I'll admit, they didn't have much flavor, but I didn't let that stop me.

I pressed on, chopsticks in hand, as if this was just a routine Friday night dinner. At one point, the person across from me pointed at the edamame and said, "Wait, Mark, are you eating *those*?!" I nodded slowly.

The entire table burst into laughter. I sat there, smiling . . . wondering what I'd done wrong.

Finally, my friend explained, "No one eats the pods! You just pull the beans out and get a bit of salt off the shell as you do." More laughter. I'm still trying to catch up.

At that moment I noticed *two* bowls of edamame. One is the serving bowl. The other was the discard bowl. This whole time, I'd been grabbing the shells they'd already sucked clean. Not only had I eaten something that wasn't supposed to be eaten, but I'd been grabbing the ones with no beans and no flavor. The salt coating had been replaced with their saliva.

My friends and I still laugh about my edamame mishap. It turns out, the edamame was a bit more complicated than I thought—and it wasn't even a green bean. Edamame are young soybeans, served in the pod. I should've just asked my questions. But instead, I decided I didn't need help and would rely on myself. This is a picture of how pride functions in our life.

At the very core of pride is this: an attitude that we don't need help. Our pride gives us an inflated view of our own self. Arrogance grows from that, and a sense of self-importance that always sees *our* way as best. Pride and self-sufficiency are linked together like two soybeans in an edamame pod.

This plays out in a lot of ways in our life. Sure, in situations like dinner with friends, but in far more consequential ways too. At its worst, our pride leads us to believe we don't need God's help. We really believe we can do better on our own! It makes sense why James 4:6 starts with "God opposes the proud," because the proud man lives his life independently from God.

The rest of James 4:6 says, "but gives grace to the humble." God gives help to those who are humble enough to ask for it. Humility is when we accurately view ourselves and our need for God's help. In our humility, we choose to depend on God as our helper in life, instead of seeing ourselves as good enough to do it alone.

Pride is so dangerous. It's also extremely difficult to identify within ourselves. We give ourselves a pass when we confess pride in a general sense. But we must dig deeper to find where our self-sufficient tendencies lie. With that kind of honesty, we'll discover our pride issues in big and little ways. We'll see ways that we think too highly of ourselves to rely on God. Ways we should be asking for help, but we don't. As we see those things—let's move away from pride and self-reliance—and depend more on God. We'll walk wisely, experience His grace, and might even be saved from embarrassing moments like I had with edamame.

Pride is so dangerous. It's also extremely difficult to identify within ourselves.

How Can I Tell If Pride Is an Issue with Me?

I (Tim) can almost guarantee pride is an issue with us guys, especially when we're young. I actually thought I was a pretty humble guy—until I got married. Sharing your life with someone tends to show us exactly how proud and selfish we are. And pride will mess us up more ways than we can count if we don't deal with it, and *fast*! Think about all people in the Bible who made tragic mistakes or destroyed their life due to pride.

Don't wait for marriage to show you how you're proud. Identify it and attack it now—and you'll be on your way to being a much better man. Here are twelve telltale signs that pride could be an issue.

We're easily offended, irritated, or angered. Pride builds a "you're special" attitude in us. When we *aren't* treated quite so special, we get upset.

We're impatient. Pride says "I'm more important than they are." How we drive is a good way to check this. When a highway lane merge causes a backup, do I take my place at the end of the line—or zoom ahead so I can slip in closer to the front? Do I honk at drivers ahead of me who don't charge off the line quickly enough when the light turns green? Do I tailgate drivers who drive too slow?

We keep others waiting. Are we habitually late to meet others? When we're crossing a street and a car slows or stops for us, do we pick up the pace so as not to make them wait for us, or do we maintain our speed? My dad taught me that a man doesn't make others wait for him.

We want to be heard. We tend to interrupt others. Speak over people. We talk about ourselves a lot. We're quick to give our opinions in person or online—and if people don't see our brilliance, well . . . they're idiots.

We put others down but expect everyone to respect us. And they *should* respect us, because we're the best.

We think we're invincible and self-sufficient. We can abuse our bodies, and we'll be okay. We can take big risks and come out unscathed. We tend to rely on our strength, smarts, or skills—instead of God.

We want recognition. We all want this, to an extent. But craving recognition and credit can be a sure sign of pride. We live in a society that teaches us to brand ourselves to get ahead. That can feed pride. I like what John the Baptist said about Jesus: "He must increase, but I must decrease" (John 3:30). He definitely had that pride/humility thing balanced. If we're more interested in making a name for ourselves than making Jesus known and glorified through our life? We're in pride's grip.

We choose the best. There are times when our taking the best means someone else gets second best. I'm not talking about the girl with the best heart for Christ. Go after her with all you've got. But in other things, do we let others have the first and best pick?

We have to win. A game. A debate. An argument. We need people to see us as being *right*—or the *best.*

We don't take suggestions, advice, or constructive criticism well. I know, we like to think we're teachable . . . but are we? Do we get defensive? If we've got pride issues, we'll reject counsel and advice from those older or wiser—like parents. In fact, we often avoid putting ourselves in a position where someone might offer us helpful tips because we don't want to hear them. We're better and smarter than them anyway. That's not only proud, it's stupid.

We're slow to admit we're wrong. Am I the first one to say I'm sorry after a disagreement? Do I make excuses or blame others when something I do doesn't turn out the way everyone hoped?

We give apologies that aren't really apologies at all.

- Do my apologies come with a defensive spirit? *"Yeah, but you did this_____!"*
- Do I say, *"I'm sorry **if** I hurt you"*? That really isn't an apology at all. It's saying that we still think we're right and they're overreacting. A real apology? *"I'm sorry I hurt you."*

What might those who know you well say about your level of pride? Let's ask the Holy Spirit to show us where we're proud—and to give us the heart to change.

64

What Does Humility Have to Do with Manhood?

We tend to see humility and manhood as distant second cousins. We know they're related somehow, but they're rarely seen together.

Why don't we think of humility as part of what it means to be a man? Maybe it's the way our society portrays humble men as *weak*. "Nice guys"—who are really losers and pushovers. If we want to do great things for God, surely, we can't be *that* guy. Or maybe we don't think of humility as a vital part of manhood because we don't know how strong humility truly is.

In the introduction to this section, I (Mark) talked about humility as having an accurate view of ourselves and our abilities, which drives us to deeper dependency on God. Humility understands this fundamental truth. *If we do anything truly great for God, it's going to be Him doing it through us.* It won't be because I'm actually so great.

There's something within men that fights humility. We want to do it ourselves. We want the credit. We want the accolades. We want people to see our strength, our knowledge, our kingdom. Our identity as a man easily gets wrapped around these things, which further feeds our pride.

Some of the best men in the Bible did amazing things because they were humble enough to rely on God for help. Their greatest victories were the times God worked through them. It had nothing to do with their own power, instinct, wisdom, words, authority, and reputation.

Think about David as he stood across from the war hero, Goliath. David didn't boast of his own strength. "You come to me with a sword and with a spear and with a javelin, but I come to you in the name of the Lord of hosts, the God of the armies of Israel" (1 Samuel 17:45).

Then a verse later, "This day the Lord will deliver you into my hand." David had an accurate view of himself and the role he played. If he was going to win, it wouldn't be about who David was, but about what God would do through him. That's humble.

Paul is another great example of humility. In 2 Corinthians 12:10 he says, "For when I am weak, then I am strong." He knew his own limitations. Recognizing his own weakness drove him to go to the source of infinite strength. As a result, Paul knew he could take on any hardship or persecution, because he wasn't relying on his own strength to do it.

When we're humble in our relationship with God, it changes the way we interact with others. It's described in Philippians 2:3 when Paul says, "In humility count others more significant than yourselves." That's not to say that we look down on ourselves, but we're constantly looking to build others up as we prioritize their needs above ours.

We only get to that point when our identity isn't wrapped up in our own abilities and self-sufficiency. When we look to God to be our source of help, we're able to see other people not as competition and someone to be better than, but rather someone to serve and love and help.

It's how Jesus was able to sit at a table and wash His disciples' feet. It's how John the Baptist was able to point all his followers to the One who was coming, the One who was greater than him. They didn't need to prove themselves by grabbing attention or being served. They didn't need their ego stroked. They were comfortable to play their role as they humbly served those around them.

The humble man goes on to do great things for God, because he's relying on God's power to make up for his weakness. The humble man treats others as more important than himself because he's confident in God's ability to work through him. This is true strength, and it leads us to be a man who loves God and people in the way we were called to do.

There are extra benefits to having a true (as opposed to false) humility. Humble men will likely build better friendships, be more appreciated on the job, and get more opportunities. Oh, and they'll likely get the better Christian girl too. She's looking for a man whose real strength is in the Lord. A man strong enough to be humble. **—Tim**

I think it's time we recognize the relationship between humility and manhood as much more than distant second cousins. They're blood brothers. Inseparable. And together, they're incredibly more powerful than most people imagine.

How Can I Grow in Humility— Without Being Proud About It?

To have a humble perspective of ourselves, some might tell us to think of ourselves as scum. In my (Tim) opinion, that's ridiculous. Let's give God some credit. He made us and did an amazing job. The "I'm scum" viewpoint often leads to false humility, which is hypocrisy.

And let's not steal credit from God. He made us, gave us our IQ and basic abilities. He gave us skills, health, our very life—and endless opportunities. When we look at the truth of all that, being proud is pretty insane, right? The real credit belongs to Him.

"For from him and through him and to him are all things. To him be glory forever. Amen" (Romans 11:36). As we grasp the truth of that verse, it leads us to the secret to truly being humble:

Gratitude. The more grateful we are to God in every area of life, the less chance we'll become ensnared in pride.

When someone says, "I'm proud of you," or "You did great, you should be proud of yourself," remember that it is God who gave you everything you needed to accomplish whatever it is that you did. If we're truly grateful, pride gains no toehold in our heart.

And God gave us the abilities and advantages that He did—not because we're better than others, but to accomplish His plans for us. That ought to make us pretty grateful, too!

■ ■ ■

Mark: I remember clearly the day my dad taught me this. We were on walking a couple of miles from the auto mechanic's shop back to my dad's house. Seemingly out of nowhere, he started talking about pride. Instead of telling me "don't be prideful" or "be more humble," he showed me how to get to a place of humility. He was like a coach giving his team the play to win the game, but in this case the opposing team was pride. I started working gratitude to God into my prayer life more intentionally. It has truly been a game changer. Try it for yourself and see how it helps you embrace humility as you realize all the ways God has helped you in your life.

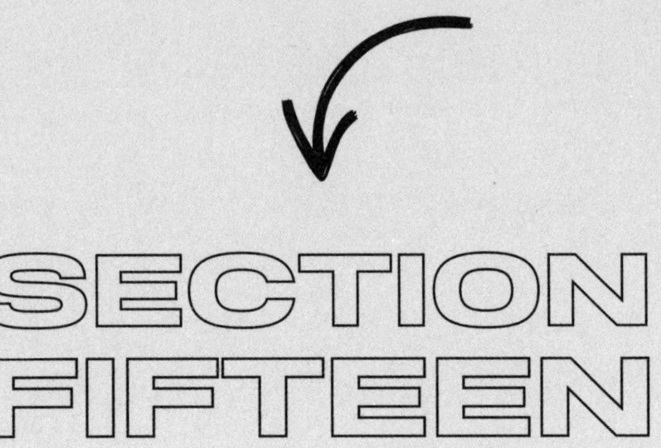

SECTION FIFTEEN

LEADERSHIP AND MENTORING

People in our culture are often driven to become better leaders. Just look at the number of books Amazon offers on the topic. Sure, we'll all lead in some areas of life. As a husband someday. A dad. Maybe as a foreman or manager, or something even bigger. So, being a good leader is important, but often people overemphasize the need to lead—and forget something even more essential. Let's tackle that in the section below.

I Don't Think I'm a Leader; Does That Make Me Less of a Man?

It seems to me (Tim) that the Bible instructs us monumentally more about being good followers than it does about being good leaders. Maybe that's because God wants all of us to be great followers (of Him) while only some men will be called to become great leaders. If God's plan for my life doesn't include huge leadership responsibilities outside my home, that doesn't make me less of a man. As men, we're to be disciples, and disciples dedicate themselves to *following* Jesus.

Even leaders follow somebody or something. The president of the United States must choose who they'll follow for advice and direction. Great leaders are usually great *followers*. Often, we see that they've made wise choices about *who* they follow.

This reminds me of what Paul said in 1 Corinthians 11:1: "Be imitators of me, as I am of Christ." He had no shame telling the church to follow his lead. What made him such a good person to follow? Not his leadership techniques or his own incredible influence. It was simply his total commitment to follow Jesus. **—Mark**

So, rather than focusing primarily on being a good leader, focus on being a good follower. When we see someone doing a great job in some specific area of life, we're wise if we learn how to follow that example. You may follow one person when it comes to advice about a career, and another about the girl you want to marry.

So, let's take the lead—and be good followers of worthy people and, ultimately, God. The better at following Jesus we become, the more we'll become the man God designed us to be, and the more others will want to follow *us*.

I Know We Learn by Experience, but I'm Tired of Making So Many Mistakes. Is There a Better Way?

There are definitely better ways you and I (Tim) can learn than by our own experiences and mistakes. We can learn by the experiences—and mistakes—of *others*. For every area of life, we can learn how to avoid nasty consequences and regrets by paying attention to what others have done—and how things turned out for them.

> ***Dating:*** You've seen the bonehead decisions other guys made while dating. You can choose to learn from their mistakes and avoid lots of pain.
>
> ***Work habits:*** What can we learn from how others work so that our work life is better?
>
> ***Manhood:*** When we see poor examples of manhood, we benefit by making sure we don't follow the same path. If your dad wasn't quite the dad to you—or husband to your mom that he should've been—you don't have to make those same mistakes.

> ***Friendships. Emotions. Dedication to Jesus. Integrity. Decision-making. Addictions. Success.*** There's no end to what we can learn from the experiences and choices of others—without having to make mistakes ourselves.

When I (Mark) was in student ministry, I'd see this play out with siblings. The younger saw mistakes the older ones made and did it differently when it was their turn. I think what helped them learn important lessons was the close proximity. They had front-row seats to see consequences play out. They saw how sin affected their sibling, their parents, and the entire home. When trying to learn from others' experiences, look for the consequences of sin. Study how it impacts the people they love and the life they live. Those consequences turn into a great teacher, so you'll know what to avoid and how to avoid it.

Here's some of my (Tim) favorite places to look at the experiences of others.

> ***The Bible.*** It's full of accounts of people who made choices—good and bad—and the results are right there in black-and-white. The Old Testament is packed too. Don't miss those stories. The book of Proverbs is filled with observations and teaches us to live wisely by examining the experiences of others.
>
> ***Your family.*** Immediate and extended. There are lots of family stories of choices made and the resulting consequences.

Friends. They're making choices constantly, and a fair amount of them are bad. Watch and learn.

Fiction . . . movies and books. I say this with caution because this isn't always a reliable source, but I've learned tons about what to do, and what *not* to do as a man based on the experiences of fictional characters.

History and biographies. These are gold mines.

We *learn* best by experience. True. And we *live* best by learning from the experience of others rather than repeating their mistakes. Let's be observers, men, and put what we learn into practice.

68

How Can I Get Mentoring or Life Counseling from Godly Men Older Than Me?

Think about your life as a road trip. I'm (Mark) not talking about a four-hour drive you can knock out in an afternoon. I'm picturing the kind of trip that gets its own playlist. A trip where you plan out which snacks you'll bring. In my mind, nothing less than ten hours is truly a road trip.

At different points, you need to make stops. Maybe it's for gas, food, a bathroom break, or just to stretch your legs. Each stop provides something helpful and necessary so that you can continue the trip—and enjoy it. No one finishes a road trip without picking up some things along the way.

That's how I view mentoring. To me, mentors are people who offer helpful and necessary things to us as we travel through life. We pick up wisdom through their experience and receive encouragement for the current stretch of road we're navigating. All of it fuels us with what we need to make it to our destination.

Here are four things to keep in mind if we're going to get the help we need from godly men.

1. Choose wisely. You don't want to receive help from just anybody. Choose someone you admire. Someone you look at and think, *I want to get to where they are*. Picking the right mentor matters. It can be the difference between stopping at Buc-ee's on your road trip—or a lone, rundown gas station. Now, if you're totally unfamiliar with Buc-ee's, imagine a gas station with over a hundred pumps and a convenience store the size of a football field.

2. Make the time. I hate taking the time to stop on road trips. I just want to keep pushing! But with good, regular stops, my drive turns out better. The same is true with a mentor. We get so focused on our goals and the road in front of us, we see it as a waste to *talk about it* with someone else. Nothing could be further from the truth.

I spent Friday mornings at a coffee shop with Paul on my day off. Early Tuesday mornings with Dale on the phone. Then there are guys like my dad, or my uncle Jim, who I continue to ask questions and learn from over meals, coffee, and phone calls. It took time to make those stops, but I needed every single one of them. Those investments became fuel that helped propel me on the next stretch of my drive.

3. Ask good questions. The first question you might need to ask is, "Can we get together and talk?" Usually, we need to initiate talks with the people we want to learn from. Then, when you get time with them, have some questions ready to go.

"How did you do ________?"

"When did you start ________?"

"What should I do about _______?"

I'd always come with questions about the things I saw going well in their life. I wanted to know how they learned to be so disciplined, or to care well for their pregnant wife, or how to be the kind of dad I admired and wanted to be. With the right questions, we can pick up so much wisdom from others!

4. Study the finished products. We can learn so much from reading the biographies of men who've gone before us. Look at their life as a whole within the span of a book, we learn from their mistakes and triumphs. Their decisions and words have a way of mentoring us long after the men themselves are gone.

■ ■ ■

Tim: We might wonder, will a man even *want* to mentor me? Men are more open to mentoring than you might guess. Titus 2 says older men should teach younger men, so God already wired them to mentor you! As long as a man feels he's helping—and that you're applying his counsel—likely they'll be glad to mentor you.

■ ■ ■

Proverbs 11:14 says, "Where there is no guidance, a people falls, but in an abundance of counselors there is safety." Think about that for a second. How often do we cruise through life on our own, just trying to get from point A to point B? Finding mentors isn't just a good idea, it's as necessary as a gas station when your tank is running on empty. So how are you doing with that? If you haven't taken a pit stop for a while, maybe it's time you find an exit.

SECTION
SIXTEEN

FRIENDS

There are worse things than not having a good friend. Having a *bad* friend, for example. Some friends may mean well, but when we think about it, they aren't influencing us in terrific ways. They're not encouraging us to make wise choices. And sometimes a friend, while putting up a front like they're our wingman, secretly wants to keep us from growing into a man who is more mature than they are. They want to see us fail. I've (Tim) seen friends like that.

This time in your life, right now, can be an especially vulnerable time. You're making key decisions that'll impact the rest of your life. We don't need friends making it harder than it already is. A guy needs good friends.

The good news? There may not be an easier time than right now to make some changes—for your own good. Because of jobs, college, or other changes, the friendship deck gets shuffled a bit. Use that to your advantage. There may be friends you need to drop or distance yourself from. And there are definitely some things to consider before developing new friendships.

To make these potential friend adjustments, you'll need the Foundational Five.

- *Remembering you're here for a reason.* You'll need friends who'll help you become the man God wants you to be.
- *You'll need self-control.* To keep from going down the same old self-destructive paths your friends may choose.
- *You'll need Holy Spirit–control.* Especially when it comes to recognizing bad friendships—and building better ones.
- *You'll need to stay connected with Jesus on this.* He knows all about good and bad friendships.
- *You'll need the wisdom gained from spending regular time in the Word, for sure.* Proverbs reveals wisdom to us . . . and helps us recognize good and not-so-good friendship traits.

Let's look at more issues about friendship.

Could My Best Friends Not Be the Best Friends for Me?

Sometimes we're so close to a friendship—that we don't realize how bad it really is. Maybe we've grown used to it—or think that kind of friendship is normal. Or maybe we've suspected a friend of ours really isn't a true friend, but it's hard to know, right?

Here are a few things I (Tim) believe we can do to help us know if our friends are the right friends for us.

Look for input. Get the opinion of someone we trust and has our best interests at heart. We must be completely honest so they can make a fair judgment. That means sharing with them what our friend says to us and what they encourage us to do. Someone older is often a good choice. They've experienced more of life. A pastor. Mentor. Parents. Grandparents. Do you know a godly girl? Talk to her. Likely she has some insights we don't. I knew a girl like that when I was your age. Eventually I married her. She still helps me see things in others that I would've missed otherwise.

Look in the Bible. There are stories of good friendships, bad friendships, and the consequences of each. By reading these stories, we'll recognize those friendship traits in our circle of friends. Here's two examples.

> *Good friend: Jonathon.* Read about that strengthening friendship, 1 Samuel 18–20, and 23.
>
> *Bad friend: Jonadab.* Read about that destructive friendship, 2 Samuel 13.

Look at others. When we see someone being a solid friend to another person, it gives us a way to measure our own friendships.

Look with fresh eyes. Sometimes we need to be honest about what we see in some of our closest friends. I heard Junior Ziegler, friend and lead teaching pastor at The Bridge Community Church in the Chicago area, say this: "Show me your friends, and I'll show you your future." It's true. We'll usually become more and more like our friends . . . not the other way around. Would our future be better or worse if that happened? If a friendship is bad or destructive for us, often there'll be warning signs. Here's a list of some of them.

> **Flattery.** Sometimes people use flattery to make us like them more—or so they can use us in some way. Flattery is different than a compliment. A sincere compliment is a form of encouragement. It is about strengthening the person being complimented. Flattery is about buttering us up—not truly building us up. Flattery is used to gain control, an advantage, or influence over another person. Flattery is a trap meant to help the flatterer gain *their* objective, while keeping us from getting suspicious.
>
> > "A man who flatters his neighbor spreads a net for his feet." (Proverbs 29:5)
>
> **Jealousy.** It may be that a friend grows jealous of our looks, personality, or popularity. Or maybe it's the relationship we have with our dad, or with some girl,

or other friends. Some friends can *seem* supportive, but deep down be jealous of some ability or opportunity we have, or any number of other things. Jealousy brings out the worst in people. That leaves us vulnerable if they have the ability to influence us—which friends generally do.

Here's something to watch for. Sometimes they'll slip—just a little. Maybe their tone of voice, or their eyes, or some sarcastic or teasing remark they make will make us wonder. Often that's all the warning we'll get, and they'll quickly cover up. We need to pay attention and not be too quick to explain away their actions. If we suspect that our friend harbors even small amounts of jealousy, they'll want to see us fail—and they'll secretly work to make that happen. Scary, right?

Bad advice. Bad friends help us justify paths that go against what God says is right. They talk us out of following the principles in the Bible. Bad advice leads to bad decisions, big mistakes, missed opportunities, lost rewards, and lots of regret.

Manipulating or controlling. Do we sense that a friend wants to steer our life—even though their own life may be in a ditch? Is a friend shaming us somehow in order to get us to do something we don't want to do? Often, manipulators play the friendship card to make us buckle. "I thought you were my friend."

If we aren't going along with them on something,

do they pressure us by reminding us of all they've done for us? There are a million other tactics. But if we sense our friend is trying to manipulate and control us? They're *not* good friends. They have an agenda that they're hiding from us. They'll attempt to get us to do and say what *they* want—with no consideration of what God wants for us. That never leads us to a good place. Many of us men who are older have learned this the hard way. The sooner we break free from a manipulating friend, the better.

Breaking a confidence. We might confide in a friend —asking them to pray for us or whatever—but what if they betray our confidence? What if they use that information against us—or leak it to someone else? There's a slogan that was used on World War II–era war posters reminding people that "loose lips sink ships." Leaking sensitive info in wartime could have some serious consequences. If we have a friend who can't keep their lips zipped, we'll take some torpedoes below the waterline for sure.

Undermining your family or other friends. There are some friends who want to eliminate others who might compete for our time and attention. They undermine those others who have a real influence on us, and sometimes in what appears to be a very humbling, almost apologetic way. They cast shadows and doubts on others who are never present to give their end of the story, by the way. They want to distance us from our family or from other friends. I call them tunnellers. Underminers. If we don't distance ourselves from them, parts of our world will collapse.

Hotheads. The Bible warns us to stay clear of those who are easily angered. They'll get hurt—and take us with them. Do we have a friend like that? If you're not sure, note how they treat other drivers on the road. How easily do they get annoyed? Are the comments they post online inflammatory? If we hang around with hotheads, we're going to get burned.

If we hang around with hotheads, we're going to get burned.

Fools. Does our friend seem to ignore what the Bible clearly says is right or wrong? Do they generally make bad decisions? Do they keep making the same mistakes? Do they ignore good, solid advice and warnings? That friend is acting like a fool, and the Bible warns us about them. A companion of fools will live to regret being their friend.

Misaligned goals. Is our friend dedicating themselves to goals that run cross grain to what the Bible says? Is it their desire to be rich, for example, even though the Bible says that kind of goal will bring much sorrow? Continuing a friendship with someone whose goals aren't supported from a biblical point of view sounds like a bad idea.

Someone who doesn't share your values—or encourages you to compromise yours. As Christians, we're to be in the world, but the world isn't to be in us, right? So, we may have friends who don't share our same values and convictions—and that can be fine. But if a friend doesn't respect our convictions and chips away at our values? Not good. For example, I've made the choice to avoid alcohol, yet have many friends who see no problem drinking. That's fine. But if one of those friends pressured me to compromise my convictions, they'd be a selfish friend, not a true one.

After reading this list, maybe you're beginning to see that one or more of your friends aren't quite the friend you thought they were. That's hard . . . but *really* good to know. It shows a maturing in you, especially if you take immediate action. If we see any of these tendencies in a friend—run. Not every person who says they're our friend has our best interests at heart. A bad friend is always costly in the long run . . . and we end up paying the price.

Now, maybe you recognize yourself in the list above. If you're not the kind of friend you should be, talk to God about that. He's given you the Holy Spirit to help you become the man—and friend that you should be.

How Do I Be a Good Friend— And Make Good Ones?

First, we ask God to help us. We ask Him to lead us to someone who'll become a good friend.

The best friends I've (Tim) known have a way of encouraging me to live according to God's Word. Not that they have to say that. I see the choices they make—and how they make them. I see how they talk. Live. It becomes obvious that they want to live according to God's Word too. When I surround myself with friends like that, we're helping each other because we're heading toward the same destination. Friends like that sharpen us . . . and they'll help us become the man God designed us to be. It's pretty hard for a friend to do that unless they're a committed believer themselves.

How can we find friends like that?

At church. They're probably serving in some way. So, get in there and volunteer. I've found that serving together is one of the greatest ways to make a good friend. Does the church offer small groups? That can be a great place to build good friendships. *Not interested in sitting around a circle sharing your feelings with guys?* Me neither. Often, a big part of small groups is about hanging out with other guys and having a good time. That's something we want. These are guys who have curiosity about the Bible, or an interest in finding out what it means to really follow God. The group leader, or someone in the group is usually all in on that, and it often rubs off on everyone in the group. High tide raises all boats, right?

Suggestions, recommendations, and introductions. We can get friend suggestions or recommendations from someone we respect and trust. Parents. Youth pastor. Mentor. Often, they see things we may have missed. They may know someone who's looking for a friend—just like we are. Ask for an introduction.

Divine appointments. I take fewer and fewer things as random. If someone is on my path, on my mind, or on my radar for some reason, I take it to the next level to see if this is a nudge from God. Is this someone He wants me to meet? Maybe to help them—and likely me at the same time? Is this someone He wants me to call on the phone? And when we meet someone new, at church, for example, we want to see if this is someone God put in front of us for a bigger reason. Let's not settle for exchanging names and handshakes. Invite them out for coffee or whatever.

Stay hungry. The search for good friends takes effort. The payoff is worth it. There are times to leave the screens behind—or whatever else has the ability to distract us or keep our minds coasting in neutral. Let's spend that time thinking—and asking God for direction for our next step.

Let's think about the kind of friend we'd like and focus on how *we* can be that kind of person. That will require sacrifice, because being a good friend isn't always convenient. Be the kind of friend who urges others to be loving and to do right things. And as you do that, ask God to help you find that friend who will be as good a friend to you—as you are to others. The more you're the kind of person who is a good friend, the more likely you'll find one.

▪ ▪ ▪

Mark: You might be someone who has a lot of friends, but do you have good friends? Early on in college, I had a large pool of people I considered friends (this is saying nothing about my popularity and everything about my socially extroverted self). At some point, I realized I needed more out of friendship. I needed people who'd sharpen me and help me become who I wanted to be. I focused on a small group of guys my final two years—guys who continue to challenge me and help me grow, even though we live thousands of miles apart.

71

How Do I Forgive Someone Who Has Wronged Me?

Forgiving someone who has hurt us in some way is *hard*—especially if they were a friend. But forgiving them isn't an option. Remember this choice line from the Lord's Prayer?

"Forgive us our debts, as we also have forgiven our debtors" (Matthew 6:12).

God has forgiven us of countless lousy things that we've said and done. He expects us to extend that same grace and mercy to those who have wronged us in some way. Forgiving someone who doesn't deserve it? That's a definite characteristic of a man who is becoming the one God designed him to be. If we fail to obey when it comes to forgiving others, we're choosing to sin. Not smart.

How do I forgive someone who has hurt or wronged me? *This* comes down to the Foundational Five. So many of those elements are needed.

- Forgiving starts with a reminder of who I am—and the kind of man God created me to be. There are things God has planned for me to do in my lifetime, and to remain unforgiving is never one of them.
- Forgiving will take some self-control. It's hard to forgive someone you'd rather slug.
- Forgiving will take some Holy Spirit–control. As we surrender to the Holy Spirit and invite Him to change our heart, He'll do that.
- As we desire to be more and more like the Rescuer who saved us—and as we seek to put the Bible into practice—the need to forgive will become more and more clear . . . and doable.

Remember, after I've forgiven someone, I need to let it go. I can't go around bad-mouthing the person, even though it feels kind of good. And forgiving means I can't harbor resentment toward them. God can help us let it go . . . something we'd find impossible to do on our own.

To forgive is to cancel a debt. When we do that, we no longer look to punish the person, or require them to make anything up to us. If we're going to get to that point, we need to let God be in charge of the debt. He is just and will deal with the person better than I ever could. When I leave justice in His hands, it allows me to truly let go and forgive. **—Mark**

After I've Forgiven Someone, Do I Still Have to Be Their Friend?

Forgiving someone who wronged us doesn't always mean we trust that person again—and you can't be true friends with someone you can't trust.

- Forgiving someone doesn't automatically make them trustworthy.
- Forgiving them doesn't change their character.

We're instructed to forgive, yes. But I (Tim) think we're wise if we don't hand them the keys to our car—or our heart. Forgiving them doesn't require us to trust them or to give them easy access back into our life. We'd want to see that our friend is sincerely changing first, right?

Can that trust be earned back? Maybe. Forgiving someone who wronged us is about God working in our heart as a man, but that doesn't mean God has worked in their heart. We forgive the person, but that doesn't mean that the friend who did us harm has really changed or wants to. If we give them a toehold in our life again, we may live to regret it. Some friends are just bad influences on us . . . and we need to stay clear of them.

That's hard, right? For sure; but only in the short run. Let's take action. Let's not drag our feet. Every guy I know who has made needed friendship changes has been so much better off. Their only regret is that they didn't do it sooner.

■ ■ ■

In most cases I (Mark) think we need to keep the door open to build trust back up, even if that means we'll be hurt again. But in some cases, the hurt has been so deep, or we have seen their poor character so clearly, or our friend has abused our trust in such significant ways, it changes the kind of friend they could ever be to us. Back to the debt analogy, I must forgive them of their debt, but that doesn't mean I would trust them enough to take out another loan.

Road Trip

Have you ever been to a stock car race? The type often located out in the country a bit. Oval track. Helmeted drivers buckled in, revving their engines. And once they've got the green flag, they're charging ahead . . . light on the brakes and heavy on the gas.

A stock car race is a picture of how most men live their entire lives. They're pushing hard, trying to get ahead, but only going in circles. And when the race of life is over, they end up right where they started . . . with nothing. If you want to go the way of the world, get ready for the oval track . . . because that's all you'll get.

Instead, we want to encourage you to take this manhood ride with God. When you put the principles we've shared with you into practice, He won't lead you in circles. He'll take you on a journey. You'll experience things reserved exclusively for men who choose to become the man God designed them to be. You'll wonder what's coming next—but in our experience—it'll be things you can't even imagine.

Sometimes the trip will be challenging. Other times, it'll scare the living daylights out of you. And, of course, there'll be plenty of exhilarating times. Like you're doing 80 mph on open roads—with the windows down. Moments when deep in your soul you'll know you're on the journey God has for you. Times when something inside says, *I was made for this.*

Will you run into traffic jams? Sure. At other times, you may get a flat or have a breakdown. You'll need to remember that God has plans for you. You'll need self-control and Holy Spirit–control. You'll need to be abiding in Christ, for sure. And you'll want to be wise enough to put what the Word says into practice. If you do those things, you'll stay on the road—or get back on it quickly.

"Commit your way to the Lord; trust in him, and he will act" (Psalm 37:5).

Commit your *way* to Him. In other words, that *journey*. That *road.* Stay true to Him, my friend. You'll never regret that. Applying these principles, especially the Foundational Five, will make all the difference between going in circles—and actually going somewhere that counts over the long haul. Don't settle for the oval track.

So, right now, do something with what you've read in this book. Take these principles of Christian manhood for an amazing road trip—one that'll last your entire lifetime. And absolutely know that we're cheering you on!

—Tim and Mark

"Be watchful, stand firm in the faith, act like men, be strong. Let all that you do be done in love." —1 Corinthians 16:13–14

Acknowledgments

Caleb Broussard—For his keen insight and intuition he displayed on October 26, 2025. We'll never forget the way the crowd went wild when your name came up. You're the man!

Emma Kuntz—For her willingness to shoot the author photos, and the way she set us at ease and made us so comfortable in the process. And thanks, Josh, for bringing her there—on a stormy day!

Catherine Parks—For embracing the importance of this book, helping us strengthen it, and championing it all the way through the process.

Mentors and Role Models—There are so many men who have deeply influenced each of us, and helped us see what manhood looked like. These men fueled our desire to be the man God designed us to be, and helped shape us into the men we are today. Here are some who are at the top of our lists . . .

- Tim: Dad, Grandpa Skrudland, Grandpa Shoemaker, and Nick Kangas. Your efforts were not in vain!
- Mark: Dad, Grandpa Shoemaker, Uncle Jim, and Dale McElhinny.

Dunkin—where we first talked about doing this book together.

Portillo's—providing a great place and food to fuel our conversations in the early stages of this book.

Parlor Donuts—where the book gained substance and weight . . . and so did we!